THE REALITY WHISPERER

The Human, The Soul & The Universe... REVEALED!

BRAD JOHNSON

ISBN-13: 978-1541394704
ISBN-10: 1541394704

DEDICATION

This book is dedicated to every man, woman and child who realizes the infinite potentials within themselves. May you live a life completely in compliment to your love and innocence of being.

"The Impossible is only possible when you validate it."

Brad Johnson

CONTENTS

ABOUT THE AUTHOR

Brad Johnson is known as the Reality Whisperer. Since 2008, he has studied a myriad of spiritual practices and philosophies through the ability of his connection to the higher mind.

Brad has explored many facets within metaphysics including psychic development, channeling, healing arts, the Akashic Records, remote viewing, ancient magick and consciousness science. He is also the founder of his own unique healing system, *"Light Circuitry Attunements."*

Brad is the author of two previous non-fiction titles and is also a novelist and filmmaker. He is continuing to share his profound extended knowledge that has been intuitively received through the page of this book, **The Reality Whisperer**.

INTRODUCTION

The Reality Whisperer is a name that came to me when I was still attempting to put a label on everything that I was sharing and offering through my work. I really liked the word "whisperer" as that represented a definition of one who could tune into the whispers of another phenomena and reveal what they are being told.

Since my beginning of this journey, I have wanted to discover what the nature of reality is all about. I wanted to explore more into what the universe is telling each of us through our actions and interactions with each other. Therefore, calling myself the Reality Whisperer felt like it fit. But as I continued to use this name, I realized there's far more to it than what I thought it was. I also realized that I am not the only reality whisperer on this planet, but there are many more. This is the reason why I wanted to title this book "The Reality Whisperer." Not only is it taking us on a journey with a great deal of knowledge that I've received over the years, but it's showing you, the reader, how you hold the capability of a reality whisperer within yourself as well.

The path to becoming a reality whisperer is quite a simple one, yet the difficulty may be the commitment in working with ourselves and discovering what we're holding onto inside. In my previous book, "Rainbow Wisdom", I spoke on concepts that would help you to unlock your reality spectrum. In the Reality Whisperer, I'm going to show you more about the potential of the human being, the nature of the soul and the connection to our amazing, reflective universe.

I ask you, the reader, to let yourself enter an open space of true wonder as you will be taken on a deep tour of yourself. All that is written within this book is designed to reflect to you your own incredible potentials, however; it will be up to you to embrace those realizations and follow your unique path to becoming a Reality Whisperer yourself.

May your journey be illuminating as you read these pages and see that greatness that is you.

May it be well with you in all ways,

Brad Johnson

PART ONE:
The Life Game

CHAPTER 1
THE SOUL & INCARNATION

Before we can look at what a human being is, we must first develop an understanding of the soul. It is the soul that is completely responsible for our perception of reality. More importantly than that, reality itself is created within the soul of an individual. This can be difficult to imagine as we open our eyes and see a world that is so beautiful and rich with life. We see other people living their own lives. We feel the nature around us with vegetation and a vast animal kingdom. And we need to stop for a moment and realize: "This is all happening inside me right now."

To understand the soul is to understand the essence of experience. If we are to consider what we could consider to be the grand creation, then everything that creation is represents creation exploring creation and experiencing itself. Well, this is the same as our own soul. It is us as a creator looking within ourselves experiencing us.

The soul is neither male nor female, nor is it identifiable through personality. Such expression are creations of the soul, not its determining factor. The soul in its purest state is a seed of consciousness. It exists beyond space, time, karma and matter. It is an observation essence functioning as a creator playing within the sandbox of creation understanding its depth of creativity. It is what you truly are.

To the soul, self is an expression of perceptual individuality. In hindsight, the soul does not see it as a self. It sees it as a totality. Why is this? It's because the soul is its own universe. A collaboration of spirit and mind together that allows the patterning of consciousness to be intertwined with the feeling expressed through spirit and thought expressed through mind. A genesis that creates the dynamic of a multidimensional universe. So what does this mean? It means that each one of us is a universe within ourselves. We are not witnessing a collective Earth, we are witnessing our representation of Earth shared on behalf of a collective consciousness agreement.

As we look at the seven billion human beings on Earth, we can understand these individuals as personal universes each interpreting their own expressions as they live their lives through an Earth they have created as soul. Therefore, we will never find a "two of a kind" trait through any one soul. It is impossible for two souls to be completely identical. It would be similar to trying to find a patterned snowflake of the same design; it won't happen.

Is this the reason why others have such a hard time seeing another's unique perspective? That's one way of looking at it, however; the deeper reason is because of societal programming which we will explore later in this book.

Does the soul have an ultimate goal? Is there something that the soul is looking to achieve? The answer is both yes and no. No, as in the soul has no sense of personal ambition or passion, yet it does have a will: the will to express itself in all forms it can. And yes, as in the soul is willful in expressing itself infinitely through the most powerful force there is in creation: Love.

There is no limitation when it comes to the soul's creation. Like a child in a sandbox, that child can create anything they wish from the sand through the will of their imagination. The soul's sand in this case represents love. Love is what creates and this is the soul's greatest tool.

The soul is not just a representation of your physical body in this lifetime, but it also carries its essence through everything that you witness: people, places, events, things. Everything and nothing combined. There is not one sub-atomic particle in all of creation that does not have your own unique soul signature within it. There is not one thought nor one feeling in all of creation that does not have your own essence within it. This is what we understand as inter-connectedness or oneness.

If we were to see creation as a seed, we are all contained within that one seed. We create a habitable environment within this realm so that the seed may prosper: this environment is the universe. Every sprout that comes from that seed is creation expanding itself through its environment. As more sprouts come together and a stem forms, we start to see the beauty of collective symmetry culminate. That culmination comes together through the billions of natural processes that are affecting the growth of the seedling through its shared environment. The environment is what we have created within to allow growth. This growth continues until the seedling is now a beautiful plant filled with life. Overtime, that plant will return to the soil as its container expires. The seed now becomes part of the Earth and a new seed takes its place from everything it has learned from the first. There it will grow, nurture and develop into an even more exotic plant.

This is creation learning from itself, just as we are learning from ourselves here and now. Understanding, deconstruction and reconstruction are the principle of what make up life. It is known as living alchemy. This is the very will of what our soul is: the will to construct, deconstruct and reconstruct again through an endless paradox that compliments the understandings of the infinite.

As previously mentioned, the soul is a genderless essence. What we understand as the masculine and the feminine are the natural hemispheres within the oneness of the soul. This means that you yourself have been both male and female beings. This leads us into the next subject relating to incarnation.

The Game of Incarnation

Before we look deeper into how a soul incarnates into a human body, we need to understand more about how a soul comes into levels above the physical plane: the astral, ethereal and causal planes. When a soul enters this universe, it exists as a non-corporeal energy that travels through the astral, ethereal and causal planes existing between the dimensions of space, time and matter. This is what's known as a sojourn.

Prior to the sojourn experience, the soul (as an essence of mind and spirit) enters condensed as our universe could be perceived as a prism or a type of filter. What's unique about our universe is that it is a cooperative, collective universe shared in experience with countless beings of creation. In other words, we're all sharing a space here that we have collectively agreed to co-create through ourselves as personal universes in a manner of speaking. As our universe is this prism, we could imagine the loving white light of creation entering this prism and seeing it reflect a rainbow spectrum. This would be a suitable analogy on how our universe is a dynamic creation manifested by all of us through such a profound collective agreement.

As the soul enters our universe via a singularity, it begins to explore the planes of existence based on what it is magnetically attracted to. Some souls can get involved with different experiments involving a collective or oversoul. Others simply enjoy the way of observation. As a soul, you are free to explore all dimensionality and planes of existence through your own leisure. It is when the soul first involves itself in a game of incarnation that its freedom can become restricted. Why is this so? It's because of the law of karma which we will discuss later in this book.

When a soul is invited by the oversoul of a certain game, the soul will enter the singularity contained within the local galaxy where this game is located. The soul will sojourn through the singularity of a host star that contains the planetary game in this example. Upon arrival, the soul will magnetize its energy upon the planetary matrix or grid. This could be referred to a sojourn check-in. Within this state, think of a drop of water that returns to the ocean. The soul now becomes one with the planetary mainframe and enters a queue where it will receive instructions based on the incarnation it chooses. It is through this experience that the soul works with the oversoul of the planet to arrange its soul or life contract. This leads into physical incarnation which we will explore further shortly.

Why does a soul choose to become an entity within this universe? An entity is known as a being of the astral planes. They exist in a quasi-physical state as a condensed aspect of the soul itself. An entity will do this because of the infinite degrees of experiences that represent a creator form. As an entity, you hold a great deal of capabilities. Entities can also hold a strong range of emotional and mental states. It is through these emotional and mental states that determine the construct of their reality. A universe is a platform that allows an entity to explore their facets of creativity through such a prism of experience. This goes back to the sandbox analogy. An entity sits in the sandbox and chooses to create as a matter of expressing themselves from within.

It is very common for an entity to become invited by an oversoul collective to experience a game. For this example, we will consider the game of Earth. The Earth's collective consciousness could be defined as the Earth's oversoul. An oversoul represents a legion consciousness of energy that exists beyond the physical planes of existence. It does not personally experience the deep involvement that an incarnate experience would. One might think of it as an administrator that oversees the game in its entirety. The oversoul decides all aspects of the game. It decides the Earth's cosmic plan, the type of incarnates it wishes to have upon its surface, its cycle of evolutionary states, its ecosystem, etc. Think of it as a grand architect that has created all essential blueprints necessary for a game like the Earth to be brought into being.

Incarnating into the Body

As mentioned in the Tibetan Book of the Dead, a soul takes 49 days to fully incarnate itself into a human vessel. Why is it 49 days? Firstly, evolutionary life operates commonly in cycles of 7. The number 7 has been known throughout the ages as the number of heaven. In this instance, it could also be known as the number of cyclic life.

The result of the seven effect (7 days x 7 weeks) allows the host body's pineal gland to become fully active 49 days after the time of conception within the host body. One could understand that the pineal gland could be the central command center, or the seat of the soul. When the soul fully incubates itself within the host body, instructions between the soul's matrix and the DNA of the fetus begins to form.

During this process of the soul enveloping itself into the body represents different vorticular activity as the soul works through a condensing of plasmatic material and light synthesis into cohesive chemical cellular bonding. As the soul integrates into the body, each cell becomes contained with its intelligent information. Like how a container would become filled with water, only in this instance it would relate to electro-photonic plasma that saturates every part of the body down to the deepest microscopic perception. As time progresses, this becomes the reason why the baby begins calibrating its bodily functions through spontaneous muscular twitches, hand and foot movements, etc.

Our own bodies are similar in how the Earth's magnetic field is oriented. We also contain north and south poles as well between the crown of the head and the bottom of the feet. This would be the magnetic and plasmatic process in the soul enveloping its essence into the case of the body through vorticular bio-magnetic integration. This flow of energy travels in and out of both poles that continue for as long as we live. Such a flow of energy is termed in different cultures as qi, ki, prana, mana or life force.

As the process of infant maturation develops, cosmic instructions are being fed not only to the baby, but also to the mother. The mother's DNA is communicating in kind with the baby's DNA representing configurations karmically between the mother, the father and the child. The mother and the father's DNA is the palette that allows the baby to configure its body, its intelligence, it's mental and emotional states based upon this collective karmic agreement. Where there may be hereditary abnormalities, should the soul occupying the child's body contain karmic history that could be vulnerable in parallel to such karma, it could inherit these traits as well.

When the child is contained inside the mother's womb, they are not as susceptible to the karmic involvement of the outside world. They are incubated within a source cocoon and are heavily shielded from much of the social programming taking place upon the Earth. The moment they are susceptible to the Earth's social mainframe is the moment that the child arrives at birth. At the very moment that the baby is fully emerged from the mother's body, an astrological imprint is placed upon the birth date and time to indicate a 'cosmic stamp' symbolizing the chosen archetype that the entity wishes to experience through the incarnated vessel. This is where the official game of incarnation begins as the child enters the world and is now susceptible to all the collective programming that will bombard it as the source cocoon has been broken.

In Review...

- The soul is a continuum of infinite expression ever exploring itself here and now.

- Everything that exists within this universe has your unique soul signature within it.

- Our soul enters this collective universe, condenses itself and sojourns to understand its nature through different games of incarnation that are available (i.e. – Earth).

- Incarnation games are by invitation only. Therefore, you were invited to participate in this game and you accepted.

- 7 is the number that governs our cyclic life development.

- The hereditary DNA is the palette that configures our body and incarnate cycle that we will witness as we mature. With that comes hereditary karma that will rely upon ourselves to resolve later in life.

CHAPTER 2
THE FALL & RISE OF THE HUMAN BEING

When our life begins, we become a part of a complex system. That system is not to be misunderstood as "human nature", but rather human conditioning. For many thousands of years, we have been exposed to a hierarchical and heavily distorted system. How could such a system become developed from beings that many believe were designed to become selfless, kind and loving?

Before we can answer that, we must understand the polarities that we hold as human beings. As a child, we have no sense of discernment. We are aligned to absorb and assimilate all wonders of our reality. We come upon this planet with a clean slate holding no memory of who we are and why we're here. This provides such human conditioning systems an opportunity to easily program our minds with the illusion of morality, sub-standard education, distracting influence and an emotionally imbalanced society. To say that life can be uneasy is an understatement for almost everybody on this planet.

Considering emotional polarities as children is what creates fissures of trauma that stays with us until we're able to grow discernment. As children leave no details overlooked, there is a sea of distortion contained within our physical bodies that has been funneled through our mental and emotional bodies. Trauma begins by witnessing an event and reacting to it based on how our mental and emotional bodies are attuned. Where there is no comfort or clarity on why a certain situation has happened, the mind and emotional states have no choice but to reference this situation as a tragedy. As we have no emotional nor mental discipline to understand why such a horrible experience happened to us, we involved ourselves with it and label it as part of our identity. Now we have created what is known as negative karma. Negative karma is simply an aspect of our own personality that we feel incapable of resolving and harmonizing with. Karma can also be referred to as our shadow self. Whatever we can't accept about ourselves or others, we have created an incredible amount of negative karmic debt for ourselves.

Considering this example regarding emotional polarities, this is what has happened to human beings within our ancient past. The negative karma has been bred by the embracing of what is commonly known as the seven deadly sins: Greed, Lust, Envy, Gluttony, Sloth, Wrath and Pride. These archetypes of personalities have caused loving beings to be consumed by this stagnant energy brought on by emotion.

The feeling of being tempted is very easy to give into. It takes a mind that has no clairvoyance of consequence. To give in and relinquish resilience and love that makes a human being the innocence that they are is to fall into the shadows of negative karma. And this temptation of illusory power has been offered to every king, every emperor and every ruler throughout history. Wherever there has been a kingdom, there has been seduction for a man to feel that they are gods above anyone else. And this feeling of superiority has caused such rulers to disregard the welfare of their own people so that their moments of glory could be the totality of their sovereignty. The people would receive scraps and the kings would receive the main courses of all that is wondrous in life.

Throughout the ages, this has been the very cause of empires rising and falling. Now we are at a time where the shift of this once distorted momentum can become healed in our modern age. Humanity is beginning to learn from its negative karma collectively and many are standing tall to act so that history will not be repeated. Whereas kings, emperors and rulers have given into such seductive temptations, we as people allowed it to happen. It has been a collective karma that we have supported by lacking the motivation to change it.

Therefore, when we come into the body and are exposed to the world, our reasoning for seeing such a societal mainframe is because of what was just previously discussed. We have all made it this way lifetime after lifetime, generation after generation and age after age.

Now that we have considered some grim history, let's take that negatively-aligned karma and see what we can do to bring it back into balance.

The Inner-Child Cycle

The human being moves into different life cycles every seven years. From the time where we move up into seven years of age, we are at the peak of our absorption as children. The basics of how we respond and how we adapt to our living environment has become natural to us. Experience has granted direction where we wish to contribute the most of our energies. We're beginning to see what themes of activity brings the most delight to us at this age. This cycle could be called the seven-year age of integration.

The second seven-year cycle is an involved-learning age. We become more involved in activities and interests that we have grown accustomed to. During this time, it's natural to see how we apply ourselves into familiar themes that mean a great deal to our excitement. This is the purest time within the many seven-year cycles because we are the ripest in understanding what we are here to become. For example, a young girl who dedicates a great deal of her time into ballet or modern dancing is at the peak of her joy. She comes alive when she involves herself with a theme of expression that her heart has led her to. If that young girl at a later age deviates from her ripe involved-learning path, she will never be at the peak of her most authentic level of excitement. The second seven-year cycle could also be defined as the cycle of the inner child. If we don't follow our inner child and disconnect from a path that has been vital in understanding our themes of enjoyment, we will become enslaved into a theme of expression that will be devoid of any pure heart state.

Consider the previous paragraph carefully. Imagine what it was like between your ages of 7-14 years. On average, this was one of the most amazing times to be alive as a human being. Go back to those early years of your life. What did your inner child want you to be? Are you living that life right now? If you're not, why is this? Spend some time with your inner child and just listen to what he or she must say to you in this very moment. See yourself as that lovely seven-year-old again and let them guide you to redirecting your energies back upon the ripe path of authenticity. This is the key to helping all of us reinforce positive karma upon the negative karma that has been imposed upon ourselves.

Our goal as human beings is to return to a state of innocence. Where innocence has been abused, it is our nature to naturally atone for that abuse and serve innocence collectively. Those who have harmed others as well as the planet always can make amends. That is how forgiving the universe is. No matter how much darkness you have placed yourself in, at any given moment you have the chance to realize what you've been putting your energy into and serve the nature of innocence.

Living as Innocence

Innocence is far more than the word suggests. It represents the purity of being. In its Latin root context, it means "no harm". To be innocent is to be free from doing harm because the essence of what you are is love in totality. Love is the very substance that we are made from. In such a game as the Earth experiment, we have simply forgotten what we are and we journey through life to discover aspects of misalignment. This is administered so that we can utilize the teachings of darkness to propel us into the light.

No one comes into this life without experiencing some degree of shadow. We all are introduced to the idea of trauma because it is this very process that purifies our being. For us to understand what innocence is, we must first see what it is not. This is where we will eventually to discover authentic nature.

Examining Emotions

As we journey towards understanding our own authentic nature, we need to look at how emotions are created and how they affect our awareness states. Firstly, we need to understand that there is a deep fundamental difference between the portrayal of feelings and emotions.

Feelings are the product of reaction. They represent our rawest and purest forms of expression. We could interpret them as genuine reactions to life stimuli. If we were to manifest a gauge that consists of green, yellow, orange and red zones, when a feeling is reacted through us, these often stay within the green areas, or at best; the yellow.

Emotions are very different. Emotions would be no more different than looking at an erupting volcanic surge of energy. When feelings have been greatly suppressed by us, those feelings become stored and buried within certain areas of the body based upon their alignment. Eventually, as we continue to bury these constant feelings, a proverbial cup of water containing these overstocked feelings runs over. This is what creates emotional eruption. An emotion is extremely powerful if we could measure its output. When you become emotional, the only moment that exists is the entirety of that emotional release. Let's imagine we're holding a red ball in our hand and we are standing in the middle of a beautiful beach. When we become emotional, that red ball and everything regarding its existence receives 100% of our focus: nothing else exists.

Compared to a feeling which doesn't entirely obstruct our awareness, emotions completely saturate our attention. To become emotional is to lower your state of consciousness. We are isolated within the walls of an emotional theme and we will not be able to leave it until we learn to realize where our attention is focused and attempt to calm ourselves down.

So, what is being said here? Should we attempt to ignore our emotions and deny them expression? Not at all. Emotions are a purifier. When you're emotional, your body is going through an intense purging of contaminated energies. One who may become extremely sad for instance can feel the heaviness of a great emotional process leave their body once they have shed tears and worked out the emotional sensation for themselves. Once the emotion has become successfully forgiven and purged, that person now feels different. They have released the overstocked feelings of that emotional entanglement and can now focus on higher levels of awareness. Like the red ball and the beach example, the red ball can be tossed into the ocean and now you have the splendor of nature to admire as your awareness levels are now bringing themselves back into balance.

Each of us have fallen through some part of our life. But what's important to understand is that no matter how far we have fallen, the element of timing will cause us to rise and work on ourselves intensely so that we can excel at becoming an evolving, forgiving and liberating human being. We will begin to examine how each of us can work with these intense emotional shadows, what happens to our soul as we become emotional and adopt the process to achieving emotional liberation in the next chapter.

In Review...

- Trauma begins by witnessing an event and reacting to it based on how our mental and emotional bodies are attuned.

- Work with your inner child to follow a pure path of authenticity.

- The way to discover who you are is to live a life of innocence, and promote that innocence within others.

- Feelings are the product of reaction. Emotions are feelings withheld and built-up overtime only to be released with intense energetic explosion.

CHAPTER 3
ACKNOWLEDGMENT, FORGIVENESS & LIBERATION

When we carry shadows with us, a part of our soul becomes divided. Every type of trauma we assign to ourselves cause the emotional body to fracture and separate from our wholeness fragmenting as an anchor attached to the woe that is responsible for our discontentment. When this occurs, we become bombarded by disease that affects our physical, mental and emotional bodies. The only method to allow defragmentation to take place and recollect these fragments of ourselves is to work towards a retrieval process. Ancient Shamans refer to this process as "soul retrieval." A Shaman is a healer of the spirit and will work with other spiritual beings to help another retrieve the dissociated fragments of their soul to achieve soul retrieval.

Our traumas are complex and intense. From this point on, we will refer to such personal traumas experienced as "karmic debt." Through this label, this is letting you know that the karma applied to yourself is not permanent and can be re-balanced. This will be our goal within this chapter.

Karmic debt is alluring as it entices us to fuel soul fragmentation to a deeper level of suffering. Much of the karmic debt we carry involves the woes of our own family lines that extend generations past. As discussed in Chapter 1, the Mother and Father can pass their own karmic debts onto their children at before birth.

Is there an ultimate cure to these traumas? The idea is not to see the re-balancing of karmic debt as a cure, but rather a sense of self-management. Where we neglect to manage our traumatic situations, the karmic debt can repeat itself. This is not a one-time fix where we simply re-balance the karmic debt and we never must see it again. We journey through life encountering new challenges and new cycles of growth. To live is to experience challenges, adjust ourselves regularly so that we can become more than we ever thought possible as an evolved being. As we grow accustomed to working with our karmic debt and re-balance the energy, our responsibility in managing ourselves becomes natural.

If we hold grudges towards ourselves and others, we will never become free from the burdens we carry. There is no pill to take and there is no method that works for everyone. Each person has their own unique signature of karmic debt. The key is to discover what type of karmic debt affects us and how we can bring it back into balance.

Measuring Karmic Debt Exercise

Let's try an exercise that may help you uncover what types of karmic debt you may be experiencing. This will give us an understanding of how these karmic debts impact you and how we can work to balance them using positive reinforcement. This exercise will assist you in understanding what areas are affecting karmic debt within your life.

As you look at the subject areas below that measure karmic debt levels from a scale from 0 to 10 (0 = No Karmic Debt, 10 = Extreme Karmic Debt) answer truthfully as this will help you to bring the appropriate amount of positive reinforcement bringing balance to your karma.

What is your current karmic debt levels as it relates to the following:

Your emotional wellness?

0 1 2 3 4 5 6 7 8 9 10

Your physical wellness?

0 1 2 3 4 5 6 7 8 9 10

Your family/friend relationships?

0 1 2 3 4 5 6 7 8 9 10

Your love/romantic relationship?

0 1 2 3 4 5 6 7 8 9 10

Your current choice of career?

0 1 2 3 4 5 6 7 8 9 10

Your financial wellness?

0 1 2 3 4 5 6 7 8 9 10

Your personal freedom?

0 1 2 3 4 5 6 7 8 9 10

If any of the above is at a level of 5 or lower, this is minor adjustment that would need to be made. If for example, your personal freedom is at such a level, consider putting more complimentary ideas into your daily routine that enrich your personal freedom further: taking an interest in hobbies, activities, creative projects. Make an entire day out of it and re-adjust how you spend your personal energy. If there's too much demand in your life, balance it out with fun, playfulness and loving compliment to yourself.

If any of the above is at a level of 6 or 7, your karmic debt is in the early stages of becoming highly traumatic. Take a break from what you're doing and give yourself some self-time. If, for example; you're feeling that your family/friends relationships are starting to become uncomfortable, take a break period where you're in your own company. Let this be a time of self-appreciation and pampering: enjoy a short trip, get a massage, dance/sing to your favorite songs or paint a picture. This is letting you know that there has been more demand upon others' expectations rather than harmonizing with yourself. The goal here is to feel self-clarity so that you can come back into the collective world with a clear perspective. This will help you to make appropriate adjustments in managing your time and energy so that the levels of karmic debt can drop.

If any of the above is at a level of 8-10, your karmic debt is within the levels of moderate, severe or extreme trauma. When this happens, put your responsibilities on pause and create a quiet, pleasant space for self-healing. For some of us who are workaholics, this can be challenging to do, but it's very important as we will only create further emotional damage to ourselves if we continue to work within a theme that's in a critical karmic debt situation. If, for example; your financial wellness is in a state of absolute chaos and you're not sure how you're going to make next month's rent or mortgage, you'll need to put your current theme that represents financial wellness to a state of temporary rest. Secondly, you will need to let yourself be calm. It is understandable if this is difficult to do, but inspiration never visits one who is emotionally overwhelmed. Don't try to think of an idea while you're highly emotional. This will not go well. Simply work to keep yourself calm and stay within a healing space free of distraction or any further tension. Your mind must be clear so that you can observe how you've been spending your energy towards a level of value that doesn't serve you anymore. Examples on reinforcing positive change within your life will be discussed here shortly, but right now, calmness is the key to clarity. When you reach such a level, refrain from giving into the temptation to panic or gravitate into fear. This calls for a time of re-evaluation that will lead you into a clear direction of resolve.

With the areas specified above, total up the amount of points regarding your karmic debt levels. With your total score, this will be a starting point where you will work to lower the points daily through positive reinforcement.

Applying Positive Reinforcement

No matter how severe the karmic debt may be, you have the capability to shrink the debt and return the areas of your life back into balance. The key to this strategy is devoting will, imagination and time to discover your karmic debt's positive reinforcement.

If karmic debt were to be looked at as a bank account, our goal would be to put positive deposits in so that the overdraft can be brought back into zero balance. As it reaches zero balance, you can continue to place long-term deposits into your account that will assist in counteracting any negatively aligned debt that attempts to come through. Through this analogy, this refers to living within your natural path of authenticity. As you continue to live authentically, you gather harmonized energy that fuels the balance between your physical, mental and emotional levels. Your life will begin to reshape itself as you continue to attract harmonious abundance and repel misaligned tendencies.

To utilize positive reinforcement, the first task is to become aware about how much energy we are feeding the areas of our energy that doesn't serve. This is something you've already done by taking the karmic debt exercise. The second task is to learn to release these tendencies that create such woes.

Releasing karmic debt is a very simple process, however; the one that's bearing these woes can make the process very difficult. As aforementioned, the strategy is to use our will, imagination and time to heal these wounds.

If, for example, a large karmic debt score exists for financial wellness, the task will be to come face to face with that energy and discover through your will what that energy is attempting to tell you. A conflicted state of financial value relates to our own personal lack of value. One doesn't see themselves as good enough or worthy for improved financial abundance and they often feel used, mistreated or treaded upon. When one's own value is in jeopardy, this will result in very stressful financial times as that person doesn't allow themselves to observe new avenues of interest that fits their integrity.

You must learn to let go of that which doesn't serve. **Surrender** yourself to this moment and release the determination of holding onto an imposed belief system. This is where you're using your imagination to transcend a personal barrier.

Releasing the Karmic Debt

Let imagination set the stage for you and visualize seeing this karmic debt as a large helium balloon tied to a string. See yourself clenching this string as you have assigned this balloon as a vital part of your identity. The helium inside this balloon represents all the stress, tension and emotional overload of this karmic debt. See this energy as something that no longer has anything to do with you. You have already become aware of everything that this energy represents. It holds no benefit to you. It's time to send it on its way so that it may leave in peace and return into pure energy. Drop your imposed responsibility for it. It no longer has anything to do with you.

See yourself loosening that grip. Feel this emotional release as you allow this karmic debt helium balloon to escape from your grasp. As you see it sailing upwards, feel the freedom as this debt becomes freed. Just allow it to sail away and return from whence it came. Feel this moment! Let it fulfill you. You are soul. You are your own universe. As a creator, you hold the key to discovering what is truly important to you. Let that importance be an energy that supports and serves you. You have the capability to become anything you wish upon this planet. Life is your personal sandbox. Let the woes go and feel the repelling and releasing of a misaligned responsibility leave your space entirely. Encourage this feeling of release. Allow it to become stronger. Take a deep breath in through your nose filling your lungs, and let the breath out through your mouth emptying your lungs. You are released. You are liberated. You are free.

This exercise is designed to helping you sink more into your natural creative power. The truth is many of us have put a great deal of energy into our own faults. We ignore and bury our moments of triumph, growth and empowerment when we still feel inadequate. Your goal now is to re-empower yourself and let what serves become the focus of your attention. Continue to use the above exercise and make this practice second nature. Document your daily experiences in re-empowering yourself. As you do, you will start to see your current karmic debt score drop as natural harmonious alignment returns to you.

How does positive reinforcement work and how exactly does our karma become transformed? To understand this, one must understand the universal laws that govern our reality. Not only will this help you to discover how to apply positive re-alignment, but you will understand how balancing the laws will harmoniously affect every aspect of your life. This will be discussed thoroughly in the next chapter.

In Review...

- Don't see the re-balancing of karmic debt as a cure, but only as a sense of self-management.

- Relinquish karmic debt but seeing it as having nothing to do with you. You are limitless and unbounded, choose what serves and let go of any debt that does not compliment who you truly are authentically.

CHAPTER 4
THE UNIVERSAL LAWS

Our universe is governed by certain universal laws that enable our reality to function the way it is. As we explore the universal laws, our goal in this chapter is understanding how to harmonize with them. Like any law that we know of, the universal laws can be surpassed once one is in alignment with them.

The Creational Understandings

Before unveiling the universal laws, there are two creational understandings that are responsible for the laws themselves. These creational understandings are not laws, but natural order that governs all of creation beyond a universal scope. These two creational understandings are:

One is all, all is one.

Now is forever, forever is now.

It is impossible to advance past these creational understandings as they are the very lifeblood of creation itself. In looking at the first understanding, nothing can ever exist outside of the one as that constitutes non-existence. Non-existence is something that we cannot fathom, therefore; it doesn't not exist.

With the second understanding, there is no time that exists beyond this now moment. The now moment is all there is and nothing can be experienced beyond the present moment. The now moment is foreverness and foreverness exists now.

All universal laws are configured to flow in harmony with these two creational understandings. No matter what universe one exists in, different universal laws may apply, but there is never an ability to bypass the creational understandings.

The Seven Universal Laws

The universal laws through this chapter are the following:

1. The Law of Free Will

2. The Law of Karma

3. The Law of Attraction and Repulsion

4. The Law of Equivalent Exchange

5. The Law of Cause and Effect

6. The Law of Space and Time

7. The Law of Love/Light

These seven universal laws work together in relationship. One cannot be created nor applied without the other. As you understand the essence of each, you will begin to witness how simple it can be to align in harmony with each. The true challenge of alignment comes from within ourselves. Our own intentions are the keys to moving into a course that serves us.

The law of free will represents our intentions and our actions. To have free will is to have the ability of choice. Every choice you make, regardless of what it is, holds possibility within you. To exist within a world of free will is to have confusion. This is the reason why this universal law can also be referred to as the law of confusion, or the law of choice.

What does it mean to be confused? Our own personal state of unawareness allows choice to become a result. We don't know what tomorrow will bring, nor the next minute or the next hour. As such, we are governed by the law of free will so that you can use your intentions to apply a selected path to see where the moment takes us.

To have free will is to be a boundless creator. No one can decide for you, nor are they capable of living your life. Such premises are impossible. You cannot change anyone, and no one can change you. Why is this? Because as discussed in Chapter 1, the soul is its own universe. You're the only one within it, therefore; as a personal universe; only you can decide on what thoughts, feelings, intentions and actions to apply throughout your existence.

Karma like anything else is an energy. This energy represents reflection based on how we define meaning in our lives through feeling, thought and action. Although karma can be defined in a negative or positive polarity, it exists beyond polarities when one considers its totality of nature. When we have negatively-aligned karma, we have simply programmed this reflective energy based on how we feel about ourselves, a person, event or thing. When we assign trauma to energy and fail to make peace with it, that energy defined as trauma will continue to follow us until one can reinforce positive karma upon it. As seen in the exercise of the previous chapter, once one applies positive reinforcement as a substitution to the once negatively-aligned karma, the energy now becomes meaningless. To refer to the energy as meaningless simply means that it no longer holds relationship to us or the life themes we explore. This is how karma becomes neutralized and reflected as harmonized energy.

The Law of Attraction and Repulsion represents the in and out flow of magnetics. That which one attracts to themselves comes through the medium of focus. That which holds no focus is repelled and contained within a state of conscious unawareness. It doesn't cease to exist, but it holds no relevant meaning in one's life. Such is the example of applying positively-aligned karma upon negatively-aligned. What's in focus determines importance within your reality, and that which is not in focus holds no importance.

Equivalent exchange governs the balancing of energies. One could see this as a scale as it pertains to our nature of value. It governs the philosophy: *"One cannot attain something from nothing. Everything comes at a price. For one to gain, something must be surrendered in return."* Equivalent exchange helps you to see your current level of value and how it has become manifested within reality. For example, anyone can truly become a millionaire, however; you must commit to becoming a millionaire in an equivalent value to that affect. If you desperately wish to become a millionaire, but you see only small amounts of worth applied through your actions, equivalent exchange will not grant you such an alignment as there is no vibrational symmetry between the intention and the action.

Cause and effect is the substance that stimulates the nature of experience within reality. Without cause and effect working in harmony, the nature of experience would become skewed and nonsensical. As one breathes in, they breathe out. As one acts, one reacts. This is the mechanism that keeps continuity alive so that you can learn through experience and understand the depths of your being within this matrix of reality.

Space and time represents a sense of property and material to help identify with linear causality. One could think of this law as the stage which life performs on. Space represents our materialized plane and time represents temporal measurement. These elements are variables serving as convenience to create relationship within experience.

Time is not the same as causality. Time truly doesn't exist. It is a measuring device that has been man-made to create anchor points or imprints as it pertains to event for the convenience of reference. Time would relate more to the mediumship of memory over anything else. An example of this would be to see yourself caught up in a barrage of flashbacks taking you out of the now moment. When you're taken out of the now, you're experience time created through memory. When you're present, you don't experience a sense of time, but rather timelessness as there's no relationship reference to anything existing beyond the now moment. In fact, if you were fully present without any interruption from memory, you would become ageless, timeless and karma-less.

Love is the purity of acceptance. The ability to accept all that is without the need to change, alter or control. It is also the living force behind the creation of all things. Love creates and nurtures, it does not alter nor manipulate. Light is information. It is where all intelligence from the universe itself travels. Inside light, profound knowledge, insight and information that tells of the universal construct can be found. One could say that love is the essence of spirit and light is the essence of mind. Together, these two essences make up the heart of our universe and reality in totality.

These seven universal laws govern our universe. However, like any program, these laws can be bent and bypassed. To align to such a nature is to become an enlightened being. One who is enlightened does not attempt to defy these laws, but embrace them. This is the essence of divine natural law.

If you can respect and honor your free will and the free will of others, you will experience liberation beyond the law.

If you can harmonize with your own karmic definitions and balance their polarities to become meaningless, you will experience liberation.

If you can work with attracting energies that they prefer, and repel energies that are not in alignment with their authentic relationship of being, you will experience liberation.

If you can accept what they experience and not attempt to manipulate the circumstances of what cause and effect are revealing to you, you will experience liberation.

If you can transcend beyond the addiction of materialization and temporal measurement and become more present enriched in feel with what the now moment wishes to share with you, you will experience liberation.

Now that you have looked more deeply into the universal laws and how to harmonize with them, the next step is developing healing practices so that you can honor the energies and meanings within your life. The final chapter in part 1 will assist you in taking down the walls of belief systems.

In Review...

- The seven universal laws govern our universe. However, these laws can be bent and bypassed once we ally and embrace them.

- Liberation happens when previous meanings have been rendered meaningless. When you harmonize with events in your life, you will bring them to balance and establish subtle energies absent of emotional intensities.

CHAPTER 5
DISSOLVING BELIEF SYSTEMS

Belief systems are the sole reason for traumas within our lives. The common expression many have is to "believe in yourself and you can accomplish anything." This statement is an incorrect philosophy.

When belief is looked at, it represents a meaning of disempowerment. Believing in one's self is not an empowering state of being. Why is this?

To believe is to have a set of conditions. Belief is not liberation, but confinement. If you believe that you can do something, there is conditionality bestowed upon yourself that prevents you from being certain in completing a task. However, when you are certain you can do something, there is no hesitation. Certainty brings empowerment as you commit 100% of yourself to fulfill a task.

This would also apply to such philosophies that reflect around hope and faith. These words are not empowering, but also limiting and confining. To hope is to hold belief that something outside of yourself will come along to resolve a situation. Faith holds similar ground clinging to a philosophy that requires obedience and belief.

The most important aspect of yourself is your own natural certainty. Certainty holds no loose ends. Yet, for one to have certainty, they must learn to respect themselves in every way possible. You must value all that represents your states of expression and interpretation.

"But, I've made so many mistakes in my life. How can I possibly be certain of myself?"

If you see everything that you have been through in the past as a mistake, you will never be able to trust yourself. By tainting yourself as a mistake machine, you'll continue to sabotage your endeavors as you will be caught up in the grip of fear. Individuals who feel guilty about their past experiences will feel fearful towards their future possibilities.

It was Albert Einstein who once said: *"You cannot solve a problem from the same consciousness that created it. You must learn to see the world anew."* Therefore, it's about renewing the way you see yourself.

When you fall and scrape your knee, you can lay on the ground and complain about how careless you were and feel guilty about making a painful mistake. Or, you can rise up, dust yourself off and keep walking as you have learned from the experience.

People have become severely programmed since childhood and the inheritance of belief is common ground. This is due to having a social system that is committed to enforcing control. The control mentality has caused belief system structures to cultivate. Your parents have enforced belief, your friends have enforced belief, your teachers have enforced belief. The influence of control becomes overwhelmingly powerful that you give into the demands. As aforementioned in a previous chapter, when you're a child, you absorb everything. Discernment has not been developed and the influence of the environment spawns the walls that create belief.

Belief is welcomed into the world culture: from morality, to religious fundamentalism to scientific atheism. The world is contaminated with this framework of mentality. So, it's important not to feel dismayed about holding belief systems within yourself. Practically every person on the Earth has them. You, however; hold an advantage as you will learn how to dissolve them.

Belief System Dissolving Exercise

On a piece of paper, think of a single belief system that you know you have and would like to have dissolved. This can be absolutely anything you wish: from something minuscule to something major.

Now that you have written that belief system down, follow the example below to get a feel of the structure that will help you to understand the belief system so that you can dissolve it.

Example: I'm a chain smoker.

Why do you have this belief system?

Smoking helps to calm me down when I'm stressed out.

When did this belief of smoking first occur in your life?

When I was a teenager. Around 15 years old.

What brought it on?

My father was a smoker. He used to smoke a lot as he was constantly under stress. I picked up his habit and began to smoke. I didn't even really like it at first, but I continued to smoke because I felt that my worries would wash away when I had one.

What type of stress were you going through?

Everyone expected so much of me. I felt like I didn't have a minute to myself. I was under so much pressure and so much demand, I was afraid I would lash out at people if I didn't have a cigarette.

Does that same kind of stress still exist with you today?

Yes. I feel it's much stronger today. I feel all I do is work and have no time for myself. It stresses me out and my cigarette is my salvation.

If you were able to resolve your stress here and now, would you quit smoking?

Absolutely.

The Dissolving Process

The purpose of the above example is to convince yourself that you are willing to resolve the root cause that is causing your belief system. As demonstrated in Chapter 3, karmic debt was harmonized by empowering positive reinforcement. This process will perform something similar to that degree.

Let's return to the chain smoker example...

Can you picture a stress-free moment within your life now?

Yes I can.

What do you see that completely dissolves away your stress?

I'm on a beach and I'm enjoying the sunshine. The sky is clear and the sound of the waves calms me down completely. Everything around me is peaceful.

Do you feel like having a cigarette in this moment?

I don't need one. I'm completely stress-free.

What does this image say to you that encourages a stress-free lifestyle?

This moment reminds me of a painting I made as a kid. It honestly feels like its encouraging me to get back into my painting again. I remember painting when I was younger and I loved it. It never occurred to me how liberating painting makes me feel.

So, in exchange for smoking, do you feel you can dedicate some time each day to your painting once again?

I can. This is something I've forgotten for so long and I know it will bring me out of this stress that I've carried for years.

What was our goal for the second half of this exercise? It was to help us find an innocence moment. An innocence moment is within all of us. It's something that we can find within the stream of our life that felt liberating. Whether it's something found within your inner-child cycle, or even within your adult years, the innocence moment is a spark of divinity found within the darkness. The goal in the above example is to help make that spark into a flame of innocence.

The image expressed in the example is a symbolism that holds a meaning within it. In this instance, the individual mentioned a calming beach. This symbolism brought clarity to them and they saw an aspect of themselves that they had forgotten: the painter.

This is positive reinforcement. As you discover that sense of joy within yourself, the next vital step is bringing that beautiful manifestation into your reality. Through equivalent exchange, the individual in the example is surrendering their chain smoking habit and receiving their joy in painting once again. This will assist in re-polarizing the karma that caused the smoking habit to propagate. This aligns with one's free will to commit themselves in applying a choice that serves them. This innocence moment attracts joy and repels an unhealthy habit. Cause and effect allows everything out in the open to the admittance of the smoking habit and the reaction to allow change bringing about positive reinforcement. This individual valued their imagination by remaining present and will create within the materialized realm something that will enrich their spirit balancing humanity and love together as one.

With this individual following through with their positive reinforcement, they have harmonized with the universal laws and will transition themselves to liberation and personal enlightenment.

Behold! A belief system has been dissolved...

Beliefs Are Personality Defenses

The reason why one holds so many belief systems within them is because they hold an external convenience to preventing our own personality from being damaged. Beliefs are an energetic barrier that attempt to cushion any sense of trauma we face from damaging our already fractured complex of identity. When a mind cannot be disciplined through harmony, it becomes fragmented by seeing vulnerability as a weakness. Pride, arrogance and ignorance are the catalysts generating cracks within the integrity of our well-being. You will never be able to experience a life full of wonder, splendor and expansion if your mind is caught up in the confinement of such personality defenses.

The common man and woman have grown up programmed to defend their ego. This goes back to the mind not becoming disciplined enough to accept criticism, accept faults or embrace vulnerability. In a modern society, some may see these as weaknesses, but that is far from being correct. Many suffer because of the resistance to embracing vulnerability. Where one falters, they feel that their identity has been irreparably damaged and it can never become healed. Yet, this is a noticeable pattern of personality defense.

A person who accepts themselves as an experiencer and nothing else will be incapable of sustaining damage. An experiencer exists to witness the spectrum of their feelings, thoughts and actions as testaments to their creativity. There is no judgment when one stumbles, there is only realization. One might also say that a pencil could never be what it is without an eraser on top. The acceptance to stumble is the strength that one adopts in alliance to prosper through life. Looking back at the previous example, when you embrace your hardships, you will discover the route to re-balancing yourself as the positive will always be able to counteract the negative. This is what is known as atoning innocence.

Atoning Innocence

No matter how much harm has been done upon one's own innocence or another's, atoning is the answer to life reconciliation. As everyone is created from the substance of innocence, the goal to atoning is to return to the restoration of such innocence.

Innocence is the epitome of purity and authenticity. It holds no fallacies to deceit or distortion of any kind. An example of pure innocence is the life of a newborn infant. They come into this world bathed with such love and care within the womb of the mother. They are without judgment and hold no desire to defend a fractured egoic personality as one has not yet been constructed through the course of time. No matter how severe your fractures that have abused innocence may be, atoning to repair those fractures are always within your reach if you're willing to apply the equivalence of love to match the equivalence of suffering.

See Yourself as Sacred

What is being said in this chapter is not an attempt for you to blindly venture through life and endure influential suffering from others. You are here to help others, but as you know, true assistance comes from an alignment of mutual cooperation. You're not here on this planet to tolerate the slings and arrows from others and be a sacrificial lamb. No, the philosophy taught within this book is to replace sacrifice with substitution.

Substitution of enduring begins with adopting your understanding of self-sanctity. One who overly endures the cynicism and distorted retaliations from another is committing an unnecessary sacrifice. Where at times, sacrifices have demonstrated resolve over hatred, a point has been reached in human evolution where examples of expansion are shown through the sacredness held from within. The example to hold and value one's own life and actions represent the greatest gift offered for others. As loving a being as you are, you are not meant to be trifled with. This is the way of spirit. The essence of a being is beautiful and loving beyond measure, however; it will not allow itself to be trampled over, manipulated nor devalued. It will leave the space of an abuser so the abuser can reflect upon the feelings and thoughts of their actions as an opportunity for self-improvement.

Let the love that you contribute be seen in a value that you cherish. Love is a beautiful energy and it is what you are in totality. Honor that energy and see yourself as that sacred being. Let one know when you feel they're not being respectful to your energy. If that retaliation continues, bow out and leave their space. Resolve cannot be achieved within a moment if there is not cooperation. The era of sacrifice has ended and the era of the sacred has now arrived. This is the substitution effect that will replace the cost of one's own life to incite an example of misaligned tendencies. Humanity can now share example through the actions of self-sanctity as an experiencer.

This concludes part one of the Reality Whisperer book. Part 2 will take you on a deeper tour as the Reality

Whisperer shares deeper understandings through the Higher Mind: From understanding your capability as a manifester, to learning how to communicate with the higher mind.

In Review...

- Belief systems are the sole reason for traumas within our lives.

- One who overly endures the cynicism and distorted retaliations from another is committing an unnecessary sacrifice.

- The essence of a being is beautiful and loving beyond measure, however; it will not allow itself to be trampled over. Stand in your light, love others; and carry yourself with respect knowing that you are not meant to be devalued.

PART TWO:
Entering the Higher Mind

CHAPTER 6
MASTERING MANIFESTATION

In part one, you learned more about the life incarnation game and how to begin yourself on a sacred journey to self-expansion. In part two, you will travel deeper and develop yourself with advanced understandings that will further yourself as an empowered human being in alignment with his/her intentions and creations.

In this chapter, the focus will be on how one can manifest as a master so that they can become clear, centered and aligned with all that they wish to embark upon in life.

Manifestation doesn't require an effort. Each of us is manifesting right here, right now. The challenge is being able to work with manifestation that serves you. In part one, you saw how belief systems are defenses for the personality. You also learned the importance of atoning to the alignment of innocence. See this as a step towards beginning with a clean slate as this is the process for you to become renewed. You are not re-birthing yourself again as you already have a tremendous amount of experience as a human being of Earth. It's important to know that you are renewing yourself, not re-birthing.

The Mechanics of Vibration

As you renew yourself and begin your journey as an empowered human being, it's important to look at how the mechanics of vibration operate.

It was Nikola Tesla who once said "If you want to find the secrets of the universe, think in terms of energy, frequency and vibration." All energy, all frequency and all vibration exists and constitutes infinite possibility within the universe and beyond. Think of it as an endless ocean where every drop of water that makes up the ocean is a single band of energy assigned with a specific meaning that is given to it by you.

A common misconception that one may make is that they put their imagination to work and wish for a manifestation to come to pass, but they are not within equal alignment of that manifestation. Another may have a set focus towards the future and wish to hear marvelous predictions for themselves through psychics or mediums, yet they take no action to allowing these predictions to come to pass.

These are states of disempowerment. When you are willing to dream big, let it be a vision big enough to fit yourself inside. One of the laws of the universe is the law of equivalent exchange. See all your manifestations that you put out through intention equal to the value that you see yourself as. Where there are differences in the scale between self-value and the value of the intended manifestation, this will only create imbalance and result in your falter. One can become discouraged if they do not take in consideration the capabilities of themselves. If they bite off more than they can chew, they will only manifest complication.

Vibration does not hold a will of its own. The energy of the universe is a prop that is attracted or repelled by the host creator. You decide how far you wish to expand yourself as well as how restricted you wish to keep yourself. You are not attempting to bargain with the universe to grant you capability: It can't set you free. You must look into yourself as you are the one that is either binding your hands or setting them loose so that they may create.

The universe is only a living mirror. It will only cast the reflections that show you how you view yourself. Every person, every place, every event, everything is a catalyst revealing to you how you see yourself in the eyes of a creator.

The resonance of energy is beckoned upon the call of relationship. When one understands the relationship they hold within themselves, they're in harmony with what they attract. Therefore, you may have had past situations that resulted in a manifestation not being able to come into fruition. There is no relationship in what you sought. And where there is no relationship, there can be no symmetry of experience. The allure to attract something that is not of your natural relationship is a result of external reality programming. Not everyone is meant to be a rock star, or a race car driver. There is a calling for you in this life that holds the greatest purity of authenticity. See within yourself all that you have experienced that resonated in joy. As you do that, these residues of authenticity will lead you to the heart of your purity like breadcrumbs spread across a pathway.

Becoming the Master Manifester

Is instant manifestation possible? Before that question can be answered, you must consider what manifestation truly is.

Manifesting is the ability to become the energy, the vibration and the frequency to bring intention into reality. One who can do this is a manifester.

Let's explore the root of this meaning. One who can **become** the energy, the vibration and the frequency to bring **intention** into **reality**. This does not mean that you are instantly going to be producing props out of thin air. This means that you have instantly shifted yourself into the preferred alignment of your choosing. When you have reached that state, you have instantly manifested yourself into a being that is now capable of bringing creation into your reality as that aligned manifester. This is true instant manifestation.

One may wish to be able to achieve these miraculous abilities within themselves instantly. That is a different type of manifestation. Such manifestation requires a great depth perception in the exploration of a theme.

As discussed, you have lived many lifetimes upon this world and on others. Throughout those lifetimes, you have explored incredible facets of capabilities. As energy always follows you wherever you go, you carry those capabilities from one lifetime into the next. Those traits that you carry are the result of one feeling that they have experienced an acceleration of capability. That's how one can excel in life. They have worked on a theme(s) that has resonated with their authentic nature, and coming into this life allows an easy revealing of that ability.

What creates a master manifester is one who can go into the depth perspective of a specific theme. Think of it as standing upon a patch of soil with a shovel. The more that you are willing to dig through the soil and explore the depths of what lies beneath, you will gain a much more profound perspective beyond the surface.

Depth is what brings you mastery. One who is willing to continuously dig and find more treasures within themselves as they continue to evolve and expand by using the tools of their already effective capabilities.

Master Manifester Exercise

Take this time now to reflect upon this chapter by going into yourself, centering yourself and discover at least three attributes that you personally enjoy. These attributes can be absolutely anything you wish: painting, drawing, singing, dancing, playing sports, etc. This exercise is to help you empower depth perception that exists within you as a manifester.

Once you have discovered these three attributes, see how they have arisen within the entire life stream of your incarnation.

- When did you become aware of enjoying these attributes?

- What feelings came over you when you involved yourself with these attributes?

- What do you feel you can do to further empower these attributes so that they can have an even greater impact on you in your life now?

In Review...

- Masterful manifestation is all about renewing yourself, not re-birthing.

- To be in alignment with a manifestation, you must become all properties within it and apply your intentions to match its frequency.

- Explore your manifestations as deeply as you possibly can. Don't give up when you only see the surface. Through depth and exploration, you will master the manifestations of your intentions.

CHAPTER 7
THE REALM OF THE HIGHER MIND

Within each of us holds the capability of communicating with our own higher aspect of consciousness. This higher aspect of consciousness represents ourselves if we were to imagine our own being hundreds of thousands of years evolved in mental, emotional and spiritual capacity.

This dynamic consciousness is something that we can access within this very moment. This consciousness can be referred to as the higher mind, the higher self, the collective unconscious, the universal mind, the Akashic records, the cosmic matrix and so forth. For posterity's sake, this consciousness will be referred to as the higher mind.

Capabilities of the Higher Mind

The knowledge of the universe is within itself. The higher mind knows nothing of restriction and is interconnected to all realms of existence. Life itself is its library of information stored within its infinite constructs.

What has prevented humankind from accessing this infinite wealth of knowledge has been the barriers of conditioning and limitation. So many of us are taught that logic is the only answer when it comes to understanding reality. This is simply not the case. Logic has its place, however; it is only capable of understanding a very minute fraction of how existence truly operates. Logic is a language that humanity has deemed as practicality. Less than 0.0000001% of reality itself exists within physical, logical practicality. If one wishes to access a higher mind that holds endless tapestries of knowledge, one will need to redefine their boundaries as it relates to logic.

Humanity has been conditioned in feeling that theories are the gospel when it comes to our reality. This is seen commonly through modern science. However, logic was never meant to be conditioned. Logic in and of itself is a physical builder that works to compliment impracticality by designing practicality through it. The essence of feeling through spirit is designed to work in harmony with the essence of logic through the mind as one. When this symmetry emerges, a human being becomes an illuminating crystal that opens all its bodily channels to receive information from the higher mind and interprets through the physical manifesting of logic and action. This is what it is to be a true empowered human being aligned with the best of both worlds both in feeling and logic.

Entering the Higher Mind State

When you are looking to enter the state of accessing the higher mind, this must come through a state of neutrality. As discussed in previous chapters, neutrality is the center point that helps you become the observer. One who is highly emotional or biased based upon self-assigned beliefs will have a difficult time receiving information from the higher mind. Think of trying to fit a large cube into a small circular opening. If the mind is not open to receive, there can be no equilibrium to allow the entry of the higher mind's flow.

Relax yourself. Relax your thoughts. Relax your feelings. The more that you can surrender yourself to the infinite and allow the flow to come through, the more insight you can receive. Most importantly, be patient in such states. Connecting to the higher mind is not a race nor a contest. You are learning to adapt yourself into the alignment of subtle vibration. When you feel at peace from within, you are aligning to the energies of the higher mind.

When in a peaceful state, simply ask your question within your mind. Once you have asked, remain patient and be mindful of how the subtle response comes to you.

Examples of Subtle Responses

- A thought within your mind.

- A vision: an image, a symbol, a word, a color.

- A voice: heard from within your mind.

- An instant sense of knowing.

- A feeling within your heart.

- Warm, fluttering sensations within the body

Trance States

There are three divisions of trance emphasized in this book. Each of these states allow you to access and receive a certain degree of information from the higher mind. They are:

- **Light Trance State**: Still conscious of yourself and your surrounding environment. An enhanced sharpness of focus and awareness. *(Beta/Alpha Brainwave)*

- **Partial Trance State:** Entering a daydream, or the feeling of grogginess. Transitioning in between the conscious and subconscious realms. *(Alpha/Theta Brainwave)*

- **Full Trance State:** Completely unconscious. Within a dreamless sleep state. No conscious recollection of experience. *(Delta Brainwave)*

Depending upon the type of trance you are in, this will determine the inner cognitive connection between yourself and the higher mind. The deeper you can venture into trance, the purer the insight obtained will be. It is possible to receive profound insight from the higher mind in lighter trance states if you are conscientious in keeping the conditional structures out of the dialogue. To become successful with this however requires a great deal of inner disciplinary training: self-trust, naturally remaining centered and having a vast sense of openness to intuitive insight.

Ensoulment

This state causes the consciousness of a host body to temporarily vacate their body. When vacated, a visiting consciousness may temporarily **ensoul** itself into the host. Another term of this state can be known as possession, however; such a term is often associated with something typically negative. This is not always the case. To experience Ensoulment, you have made an energetic agreement with another consciousness and have agreed to vacate your body for a short amount of time so that the visitor can use your body often for communication purposes. This is a rare state to witness, nonetheless; it is possible for some full trance mediums and/or channels to enter Ensoulment.

Tips to Entering Deeper Trance States

Begin by following the rhythm of the breath. Think of nothing else. Take a deep breath in through your nose and slowly out through your mouth. Repeat this intake and outtake of breath several times. Next, take a deep breath in through your mouth and out through your nose. One again, repeat this form of intake and outtake several times. Repeat this changeover continuously focusing only on the breath.

Let your body become as relaxed as possible. If you feel that you are not quite relaxed sitting in a chair or on a floor, lay on a couch or a bed. Follow the breath and imagine that each breath you take in, you are tensing your muscles. With each exhaling breath, release the tension of all of your muscles. Repeat this several times as you become conscientious of how your muscles feel when fully tensed and fully released. After you have done this, just imagine your body melting into the couch or bed as you become more relaxed and calm.

Begin a countdown from 100 to 0. As you begin to slowly countdown, feel your body and breath relaxing more and more. Make each number that you say aloud or in your mind feel like the most liberating sensation ever felt when expressed. By the time you make it to zero, you are completely centered, calm and receptive to the higher mind.

Entering Trance

Depending on the type of trance state you enter, you may not be conscious relating to what you receive through the higher mind. Give yourself a preparatory measure to document your experiences accessing the higher mind. You may want to record yourself with an audio recorder or video camera. Or you may want to have someone with you as you drift off into deeper trance states and they will record communicative experiences for you.

Remember, every single one of us drifts off into trance each night that we go to sleep. Everyone has the capability of entering trance. It doesn't have to be a fearful state to be in. The difference in working with trance as that you are becoming conscientious when you enter these states of consciousness rather than being unconscious. Ancient mystics refer to these deep trance states of meditation as "conscious sleep."

Should you feel any discomfort or anxiety about entering these trance states, explore such fears and work to harmonize with them as explained through the earlier chapters of this book.

Experiencing the Higher Mind

Each person's experience with the higher mind will always be different. Some may enter a deep state of trance and sense themselves entering a vast library of information where endless shelves of books surround them. Others may experience an illuminating being of light that holds all intelligent information and serves them as a guide. Whatever may be your experience, it is a translation of energies that fits in relationship to how you access universal information.

The higher mind truncates itself into your level of comprehension. It works with your own psyche to giving you an understanding of where you are and what you can access based upon its choice of relationship interpretation. Embrace and accept what you experience through the senses. Do not concern yourself upon what another may encounter and feel you need to duplicate them. Be genuine and unique to yourself and let your own higher mind speak to you in these realms of consciousness authentically.

The Long-Term Effect

The more frequent you're able to connect with the higher mind, the more you may realize that such deep states are no longer necessary. It is possible to connect with the higher mind in natural states of consciousness. When you enter a deep trance state, your body is being worked on through the higher intelligence: neurological pathways are being reconfigured, synapses are firing, DNA is activating, your energy body is re calibrating. Overtime, you become a natural living crystal of information. You'll see how your personality will become enhanced as you have conversations through natural flow. It will be so subtle and effortless to you, you will be amazed at what you are sharing with others. Such is the case with the author of this book.

Forming a relationship with the higher mind and making it a part of your daily life is the key to amalgamating the inner and outer worlds together. You'll notice that it will become easier to connect with your own inner guidance as you have attuned the physical and higher minds together as one.

You were designed to become this crystalline vessel of infinitely intelligent information. The more that you can work with yourself, commit yourself to accessing your higher mind and living genuinely as the intelligent information provides, you will become the vibration of that loving higher aspect of being. Continue to practice and work on yourself daily, and you will begin to see results stand out as the days, weeks and months go by. Keep a diary handy and document your challenges, discoveries and triumphs each day. As you do this, you can look back upon your progress to see for yourself how far you've come.

In Review...

- The higher mind can also be referred to as the higher self, the collective unconscious, the universal mind, the Akashic records, the cosmic matrix, etc.

- The knowledge of the universe is within itself. The higher mind knows nothing of restriction and is interconnected to all realms of existence.

- When asking questions to your higher mind, be mindful of the subtle responses you may receive as these are confirmations of reply.

- The more you form a relationship with the higher mind, the lesser you will need to enter deep states as your connection is now becoming a larger part of your reality. This is the effect of bringing the inner and outer worlds together: they will converge.

CHAPTER 8
THE WILL OF NATURE

Nature holds a will. This will cannot be understood by a rational means as true will holds essence within irrationality. Yet, the epitome of how we experience life in the totality of our individualized selves and our collective consciousness are all portions as it relates to this will. Will does not represent an agenda, it represents a flow. A gravitation as it were that represents a current to expansion. When we look at the compliment to will and the stagnancy of will, we arrive with polarized concepts.

To experience a resistance or stagnancy of will holds a cycle of contraction. This doesn't represent anything evil nor derogatory, it represents one's own concept that their aspect to contract is to see what can be released. Upon releasing stagnancy comes adjustment towards a path of natural will.

Expansion is a result of what has been released from reflection. What you're able to see and understand while in contraction becomes the effect of expansion generating greater clarity within. Through expansion, life becomes an experience of compliment, compatibility and advancement.

What causes the inception of going against the current of nature's own will? The culprit is confusion. Confusion takes you into a journey where you feel unaware or absent in guidance. This is a side effect of breaking away from belief. If you hold a system of belief, you follow the energies that the belief contains, even though it is not natural guidance. When a belief is questioned, or misunderstood, this warrants confusion. One doesn't know what to believe in and holds no grasp of certainty within their life, and so they remain at a crossroads.

Those who remain upon the crossroads can often become desperate. This desperation leads to attachment. Attachment welcomes in the assignment of belief. Now faith is acclaimed to help one move forward, yet; the movement becomes heavy with resistance because that person hasn't acclaimed the trust that grants natural certainty. Without entrusted self-certainty, there can be no known path of compliment and compatibility.

This has led to polarized concepts infused with belief. This is what has generated the energetic of polarity not only upon our world, but throughout the universe.

Incarnation Beyond Earth

As discussed in Chapter 1, a soul is a traveler. Each soul has sojourned through many different galaxies and star systems. Therefore, in understanding such a principle, the universe is teeming with life containing souls occupying other bodies on other planets and different levels of dimensions. Extraterrestrial and Extradimensional life is common throughout the universe.

The will of nature flows through everything: from the microcosm to the macrocosm. All life represents the essence of experience within the universe. Our own star system contains life on other planets, moons and celestial bodies. Worlds that once contained an enrichment of life but are now scarce of indigenous life.

The game of Earth is a 100% free will planet. Having this rule applied, confusion is granted through such an alignment, and the only remedy to confusion is the ability of choice. This is how our game of incarnation functions. But on other worlds, different rules may apply.

One may surmise that because there is intelligent life beyond the Earth, those societies must be exceptionally evolved. This is not always the case. Even though there have been some tremendous technological and spiritual achievements attained by other civilizations, they are working through their own challenges. If it were assumed that all life beyond Earth held such immense spiritual discipline balancing polarity, the neighboring celestial bodies in the star system would still be ripe with indigenous life. Yet, this is not the case.

Many civilizations go through intense cycles of transformation that hones their established states of evolution. Some civilizations have had a greater restriction to free will in comparison to humans of the Earth. This is because each game of incarnation has different themes of expression to them. Imagining each incarnation game as a school can best give an understanding about how certain civilizations evolve.

For example, there are civilizations that exist that have absolutely no concept regarding emotion. Their culture has been raised to openly express their hearts without suppression. Such a civilization wouldn't utilize any type of emotion because secrecy of character doesn't exist within their society. Therefore, this creates a different archetype as it relates to a free-will principle. Intervention of other civilizations beyond their world could be embraced and welcomed as there is no appointed governance for the secrecy of extraterrestrial life. Strangers from other planets would be as welcome as strangers from other lands. The culture is open to such experiences and dedicated to learning about different extensions of their own being that these extraterrestrial and extra-dimensional civilizations represent.

Of course, civilizations that hold a very strict hierarchical structure exist. Such civilizations are more driven towards emotional attachment and the need to control. These civilizations do not seek open community relationship, but tend to dominate and conquer based upon a "survival of the fittest" mentality. They despise free will as to grant such a concept is to allow dismantling of a control agenda.

Looking at these two examples creates two extremes: an open society that welcomes others to form harmonious community, and another society that upholds strict conditioning and control agendas warring to establish dominance and conquest.

In ancient times, the Earth has connected with a variety of different civilizations of these alignments as well as others that exist within the middle of the spectrum. This can be verified by researching a great deal of ancient civilizations and their gods/deities. Humanity was not the first race to walk upon the surface of this planet, and it will not be the last either.

As nature has will, will can only be understood through the contraction that grants the expansion. The expansion reaches a certain point, and contraction once again visits. Such is the case with the natural flow of the Earth: cycles of day and night, the seasons, the waning and waxing moon, etc.

One is not here on the Earth to merely expand. Like the lungs, you must breathe in and out to live. Therefore, you must contract to expand and expand to contract.

Within reality, one and the extensions of themselves all hold a contrast of polarities. There will be days where you'll feel on top of the world, and others where you'll feel beneath it. This is flow of natural will. The incarnation games of many worlds follow this very cycle, only through varying degrees that allow the culture to understand itself uniquely.

There will come a point where humanity will be introduced to its family that extends beyond the Earth. However, as our culture has been raised with a great deal of restriction and conditioning, humanity will require a softening transition to grasp the concept of other life beyond the Earth. Like how one would feed their young infant liquid food before they can handle a large solid portion. The collective consciousness of the Earth understands this transitional process and will facilitate the flow of events that will compliment this arrangement of evolutionary progression. Such times will start to become more noticeable in the years ahead as humans are on the cusp of being introduced to other civilizations.

The interesting alignment of the universe is that it has been known to be very slightly biased towards an evolutionary path of unity. No matter how polarizing a situation may be that represents suppression, injustice or manipulation, the stagnant resistance will only be able to run its course for a certain time until it is exposed by illuminating expansion and awareness. When this occurs, the stagnant systems become deconstructed. Once you can overcome an obstacle and see its areas of vulnerabilities exposed, you will never have to repeat that process again. Realization is the substance of the biased nature of our universe. When stagnancy's root source is uncovered, correcting the flow of resistance is unavoidable.

When you ally with nature, you can receive the most support by all life naturally harmonized to the vibrations of love. Resistance through negativity and conflict hold a tighter only because they wish to be learned from. Darkness is a teacher, not a punisher. The only punishment factor one may feel devoted to darkness is their own will to walk a path of deep resistance as if there is no other way through life. Their punishment becomes self-imposed and they exist in darkness a slave to fear, aggression, anxiety, despair and chaos. There is a desire to control when one is confined in darkness. Yet, control is nothing more than a deception. The need to control represents a fear for one to live, rather; they intend only to survive and abuse their thoughts and feelings through sacrifice oblivious that in any moment, nature will welcome them back with loving arms. It is never too late to leave the heavy grain of resistance. Surrendering one's self to the catalyst of acknowledgment and forgiveness are the steps towards aligning into a universe ready to serve and support you.

Darkness and shadows' single purpose is to educate your choice in experiencing misalignment. Where there is a failure to attune based on what the misalignment shows, the shadows of superficiality becomes one's reality. This all falls into place when it comes to one's perception of deserving. This is a reminder to remain aware of your own alignments of authenticity so that shadow can remain a teacher and not a life punisher.

This will be the focus of the next part of this book as we explore teachings that will assist in bringing expansion mentality into your life.

In Review...

- Contraction cycles are a time of great inner reflection. Expansion cycles are a result of what has been learned from reflection bringing broader clarity.

- Confusion is the culprit when attempting to go against the current of nature's will.

- Every game of incarnation has specific themes attached to them. All civilizations evolve themselves differently based upon the rules of a certain game. In Earth's case, free will is 100% available on this planet, and this grants confusion remedied by choice.

- Darkness and shadows' single purpose is to educate your choice in experiencing misalignment. It is a teacher. Once you learn that it is a teacher, illumination from restriction will become your next step.

PART THREE
Expansion Teachings

CHAPTER 9
THE ROAD OF PASSION

What brings the benefit of following a path of least resistance and becoming a servant to the will of nature involves the motivation of passion. Passion is the elixir to living a life that compliments ourselves, others and our environment. Passion is the life force that brings substance to our will to create. It is the single greatest tool that will align you onto a path that is truly your own and promote authenticity to the actions you apply.

The biggest challenge one may have is being able to determine what their greatest form of passion entails. Passion after all does not have a voice, nor does it have a body. It must become your voice and it must become your body. It is something that reflects such a bright light of yourself and it is an energy that can be expressed only by you. No one else on this planet or within creation has the type of passion and creativity you have. But to apply passion, you must first discover what your passion isn't before realizing what it is.

Therefore; our lives are truly gems in disguise. No matter how much pain and conflict has existed, these are all shadow teachers showing you misalignments that are ready to become aligned once you realize the messages they are attempting to teach you.

The most challenging thing about passion is that it is indeed a jewel hidden within the cloak of shadows. Life experience discovers it and brings it to life.

How to Discover Your Passion

It is common to find many people living a life that is not their own. It is also common to find many people wishing they had the power within them to change it and live within a reality complimentary to who they are. The greatest secret is that all beings possess such a capability to become whatever it is that they wish, but social influence and programming become their gospel and they remain lost and confused inheriting thoughts and beliefs that were never theirs to begin with. These thoughts and beliefs isolate themselves from a reality of infinite possibility and exploration. Like what was demonstrated in an earlier chapter, you have the capability to take down these barriers of thoughts and belief by re-validating what's important to you.

Hesitation and apathy are programs influenced by a control grid. You can see it, hear it, taste it, touch it and smell it for as far as modern society stretches its influence. The key to discovering your passion is the complete transcending and disassociation of influence involving modern society as possible. Your passion can become anything you wish It to be that speaks authenticity to you, but you will not find it within a programmed matrix created to keeping you at bay with adopted thoughts and beliefs. The grip such a matrix has on you must be released, and to do that requires your disassociation and lack of obedience to such a program.

Anything that is meant to disempower you and causes you to feel inferiority within your being is meant to be discarded. This involves reinventing our reality and custom-building a life that exists complimentary to what our true passions dictate.

To many, this may be easier said than done as so much of our time has been invested with friends, family, education, religion and career that has created an in-depth sense of identity within. This can be the most challenging set of hurdles to overcome. However, the will of what is complimentary to you through passion is the driving force that makes you who you are as a spiritual being. The ties you make through such inner circle relationships are supporting foundations that govern the energies you have deemed as valid. In other words, when one hates themselves and has established a relationship with other people who hate that person and themselves also, this has become so due to the one's own validity of perception. Those people that were attracted into that person's life did not come from outside, but magnetized themselves into that person's life because of how they feel about themselves. Through the law of attraction, hate attracts hate and love is repelled by the attachment to personal hatred through the law of repulsion.

What does this mean? It means that what you consider valid in life shall always be the result of your reality. Validity is consciously and subconsciously bonded. A day where you may not feel emotionally imbalanced may still bring imbalanced manifestations into your reality. This is due to the belief systems that validate your own emotional vulnerabilities and tendencies anchored into the subconscious mind. As discussed earlier on in this book, only realization, acknowledgment and forgiveness are the catalysts to dissolving a belief system so that the replacement of that belief can be generated into an alignment that serves you via positive reinforcement.

Passion becomes the result of that reinforcement. The drive to return balance back into your being by obtaining an epiphany of what is the resonance of your most heartfelt intention and authentic action. In the earlier example regarding the cigarette smoker. By him realizing that smoking was only a cloak that he held onto as an escape for stability, he looked within and discovered the most exciting aspect of himself which portrayed itself as the passion of painting. He then realized that smoking was no longer the answer, acknowledged this strength, forgave it by giving himself permission to explore what brought him peace of mind and an authentic expression of joy. Therefore, through such actions, his passion was discovered.

This is the road to passion. Reinventing your values and aligning them to what truly serves you rather than continuing to indulge beliefs forged through superficial manipulation. To truly walk this road of passion is to correct all areas within your inner circle support system so that the support itself encourages passion to be engaged and maintained for as long as it drives you.

Passions can certainly change as well. Some can last a great deal of time, and some are only temporary to set you upon a path of something even more exciting. What is important to understand, however; is that passion serves up to a specific point where positive reinforcement has fulfilled its purpose to re-balance your energies. Positivity is a counter-balance to negativity. Once it has served, passion will no longer become a driving force in your life, it will become fulfilled. Therefore, humility will follow the expression of your passion. Humility is the result of you simply being in a space of natural appreciation, compliment and authenticity with yourself. No actions of a positive nature need to be exercised because your energies have brought you into a humbled content. This shows that passion is and always will be the precursor to the alignment of humility.

In Review...

- Passion is the life force that brings substance to our will to create.

- When you transcend the boundaries of modern society's rules of distortion, your passion will be at its strongest.

- Passion only serves to a certain point once the theme you explore has reached its completion. Remember, passion can be shortly lived as you have brought humility to a theme of exploration.

CHAPTER 10
GOVERNING PERSONAL ENERGY & EMPATHETIC ALIGNMENT

When we begin working on ourselves, the excitement we feel can bring our energy levels to working at a maximized level. When we begin to follow our passion and we have worked out our superficial mindsets that do not serve, it is common to find ourselves going full throttle towards the journey that we feel the most passionate about.

Excitement can indeed be a very wonderful thing, however; it's important to realize that going into such vibratory states can also cause one to overlook themselves and what it is that they personally wish to obtain. Think of it as a machine that produces so much power and there is no gauge to show when the machine is about to go off into the red and break down.

The understanding that is set here is to govern personal energy as it serves you authentically. When excitement and passion is observed, it is an energy that is thrilling and addicting. Like how one would indulge in a favorite meal or a dessert. But there is an overage where one may want to eat too much and face repercussions because discernment was not shown. Therefore, using discernment is as much a catalyst of entering one's own authenticity than excitement itself.

For instance, you may have an interest in wanting to help another financially. Perhaps this is a person is a relative or a long-time friend. They have lost everything and seek help. Out of loving compassion, you welcome them into your home and you begin to take care of them. You feed them, give them shelter and even offer to buy them a great deal of gifts. It makes you happy that you can do such things for them and lend them a helping hand. But what one may not realize is how the other person is feeling. Because they are aligned to a state of loss, they exercise no restraint into receiving kindness to such a degree that they now form a dependability on you. When the time comes when nothing is being reciprocated through equivalent exchange, you begin to grow irritable on how your home is not being maintained, your food is being constantly eaten and your money is being constantly spent by this person. This creates imbalance in the relationship and you spend your days arguing with each other until a line is crossed and a bridge is burned. Out of anger, you expel the person from the house and they resent you for casting them out like everyone else before you. All that is left is hurt feelings, animosity and great sorrow.

What happened here? You offered so much kindness to this family member or long-time friend, and in the end, a divide was created that manifested hardship between two people. It's because there was no sense of discernment nor respect for where you both were. One was careless to provide endlessly and the other was careless to receive endlessly.

In this example, the person that was being helped came from a world where they were at a point of loss in life. They didn't feel cared for, but what it really meant was that no one was willing to help this person because they were constantly taking and not giving back. You in this example represented someone who was aligned to serve and receive joy out of helping another in need. You wanted to feel responsible for another and help to change them so that they could become someone who could take care of themselves by seeing kindness as an example to reciprocation. Neither party offered any sort of balance to each other. One gave and one took. Where was the restraint? Where was the discernment? Where was the equivalent exchange of reciprocation? There was none.

When you work with energies of passion, excitement and positivity, it is not uncommon to see many indulge in giving like what had been explained in the above example. It feels wonderful to give to another and to help another out. This produces a great deal of happiness in one's self knowing that they can be of assistance. But, where there is no feeling of discerning your personal energy and governing how much to put into a situation, an overage can occur. What does this overage do? It overwhelms the situation where the alignment of fair balance becomes extinguished. An overage of kindness and generosity meets with an overage of taking from another and leads to dependence. You are the savior in that person's mind and they don't have to feel responsible for themselves as they see you as a provider. The overage offers no opportunity of reciprocation in any form, only a usurping of energy until a threshold becomes crossed and raised emotional tension fills the air.

When one cannot govern their energies, they will become careless of the type of alignments they attract as a result. Kindness is a wonderful thing, but providing it exponentially to one who has suffered can lead to an overindulgence that fuels the alignment of undeserving into dependability.

What represents an example of governed personal energy? Going back to the previous example, one who has felt they have lost everything Is counseled to helping them see what can be attracted through them as a resolution to their despair. Empathetic assistance is given to show that you are there for that family member or long-time friend. Not to look after them by feeling responsible for them, but encouraging them to find their own answers with what the situation of loss has brought to them. Allow them to find their path by living through the example of its opposite alignment. Be there for support, but do not feel that you must give so much to them when they are in an alignment of sorrow and defeat. It can't be reciprocated at this stage because they are feeling unworthy and are in a lack of value with themselves.

Encourage their emotions to come out and feel what they genuinely feel by holding space for them. This can be the greatest favor you can do for one who is suffering. Be one who loves and listens. When they have the space to emotionally release with the care of a family member or friend, they will awaken in time and realize what they must do now that the emotion has been released in a space without judgment.

The Balance of Energy & Vibration

It is common for many of us to push the envelope when we first encounter excitement and passion in what truly feels authentic to us. What is important is what we learn through experience that helps us to adjust how to best utilize and conserve our energies. Yet, the greater awareness you hold with managing your own feelings and discerning the elements of a situation before you act on it, the more that you can go at a speed that is comfortable that flows in excitement without the risk of going into the red.

We are a conduit of energy and vibration. We govern our reality and solely determine where we contribute our energies in the face of themes we choose to explore. Without evaluation of what those themes hold for us through meaning, our energies can intensify such a theme where we face repercussion for careless lack of discernment. It is wise not to rush into a situation without being able to understand the connections the facets within it hold. Like the example of the friend who faced loss, it can be very easy to falter with energies we believe to be of service when in fact it can be detrimental to you and the other.

You are a catalyst to every situation because each situation is connected to all things within reality. Nothing is ever unrelated, unnoticed or unaffected. Our actions are projections of energy that emanate throughout all that we sense expanding throughout the cosmos. Only one who is responsible for their actions and intentions behind them will learn appropriate governance and reach enlightening understanding. It is no easy task as haste is often the demise we face when met with a strong will of ambition.

When we observe a life situation by looking at the people involved and how they are entangled through the dramatic theme, we discern for ourselves to determine if such an endeavor is worth the contribution of our energy. Many times, we become involved because of emotional tendencies such as: pride, loyalty, ambition and dependability. These are nothing more than drama-influenced justifications that are set traps waiting to go off as we equate to indulging on an emotional level not yet purged from us to see clarity. Thus, we become indulged in going through an intense dramatic period as a way of seeing what we carry that has shown imbalance. In this instance, this is called going through a dark night of the soul. Our shadow wishes to present itself so we can notice it, forgive it, liberate it and become as one again in harmony.

Aligning to Empathy

Empathy is one of the greatest tools within the capability of mankind. It is so powerful in fact that generations of control systems have attempted to breed it out of every man, woman and child. If the entire world was filled with deeply empathetic human beings, we would exist on a planet so breathtakingly beautiful, it could not be described by mere words. Can you imagine a world where fellowship, community, compassion, love and cooperation would be commonly shared among everyone? The compassion would not only extend through human experience, but our very environment itself. Animals would be our counterparts assisting us in purifying the lands and oceans. Nature would be a major part of our life as we learn to exist more prosperously through what it offers in terms of shelter and abundant food as well as natural medicine. In fact, if everyone were empathetic, we would no longer have extreme weather or tectonic conditions upon the planet as such things are reflections of mankind's emotional extremes and programmed opposition towards nature favoring technology. We would never think to harm our children with genetically modified food, or drug each other to maintain emotional numbness and apathy. There would be no wars or poverty upon the planet whatsoever. All of this and more would be possible because we have aligned ourselves to become empathetic and show our hearts to each other openly without condition.

This is what Empathy can do for us and the planet. This is the true nature of our spirituality. When you learn to open your heart to levels that reflect a 100% daily compassion, you will witness an incredible reality reflected to you. Empathy is the true spice of life. The ability to feel each other through our hearts, minds and souls all by having the ability to care for one another. It is one of the most powerful and beautiful gifts to ever offer another being.

There is no excitement with apathy. Apathy numbs our ability to see the depth within reality. You become surfaced with the world around you alone with thoughts of carelessness. Your energetic centers will eventually shrivel and atrophy due to such a suppressing numbness and that can cause overwhelming states of dis-ease. Expansion cannot visit you where there is apathy and numbness. You only continue to align yourself into personal confinement and withdraw from all that is truly beautiful and magnificent in the world.

Is there a powerful method that will align you to empathy? Absolutely.

The powerful method is the ability to smile. This does not mean that you are smiling only because you feel you need to. That defeats the purpose. Do not prepare for a smile or schedule yourself to smile. That is forcefulness and that does not equate to the alignment of true joy.

What can you do that can give you the authentic ability to smile naturally and frequently each day?

The answer is a space of love in yourself and in your environment.

Your environment is a vital part of how you reflect yourself through reality. Your home, your office, all your surroundings-- Align it to something so joyful and beautiful, you feel that you're going to melt each time you take it in. Let your soul out upon the walls of your space. To do this, go back into your inner child. Like what was discussed earlier on in this book, your inner child is the most creative aspect of yourself as it holds the purity of innocence within.

Your space of love holds no judgment of itself. It does not apply conditions to its own unique expressions. Therefore, make the ridiculous, the crazy and the childish a part of your life as much as possible. Spontaneously dance in the silliest of ways possible, try your voice with singing a tune or chanting, crack a joke that you haven't heard in a long time that will make you giggle, paint a beautiful picture filled with colors. These are all powerful expressions that will not only make you smile, but make you laugh and truly enjoy yourself.

Every time that you crack a smile naturally, your heart expands a little more. Every moment of laughter that comes out of you, empathy has grown just a little stronger. Feel that inner space of love within yourself where your inner child is the host of that space. Make each day of your life a party that celebrates how beautiful you know yourself to be through the authentic expression that can only be shared by you. This is the alignment of empathy and this is what can bring a vastness of depth into your reality. If you wish to understand the nature of your own universe, it begins with the ability to care for yourself, for others and for the universe itself.

In Review...

- Passion and excitement are powerful stimulators, but must be governed by personal discernment to balance the symmetry of your manifestations.

- Watch your actions and behavior as you interact with others within your world. Other selves can tell you a great deal about how you perceive yourself from their perspectives. Such observations are telling you truly how you see yourself.

- Be aware of the power of empathy. Empathy and kindness are the energies that can profoundly transform your world unveiling more possibilities within it.

- Most important of all: smile as often as you can.

CHAPTER 11
WITNESSING & PERCEIVING WORLDS

When one looks at the concept of the world, they are looking through a looking glass that cannot be changed, manipulated or controlled. The world as it is understood is the result of looking at a vast extension of one's own subconscious. Yet, this extension of subconscious is only meant to be observed and witnessed. It holds an incapability of being interacted with.

Think of an interrogation mirror within a police station. The detective is watching the subject through the mirror studying them as the subject believes themselves to be alone. There is no connectivity of involvement at work. There is simply the degree where one is witnessing reality without involving themselves with it. To see reality in this way is to be a witness of it. No attachment, no possession and no involvement of circumstances.

Why would one wish to simply witness their world? What exactly does this bring to ourselves? To be able to witness the world before you is to hold a state of acceptance of how everything exists. In this state, you are not creating by intending. In a state of witnessing, there Is no demand of your energy to focus, concentrate or to think. It encourages you only to be aware of what exists within yourself.

Witnessing is the closest understanding we have as it represents the alignment of love. Love in its purest state is the ability to accept, honor and appreciate all that is as it is. When you are truly in a love state, you do not wish to change anything. You have no desire to do, or to have, or to want or to need. You are simply in the alignment of witnessing by being still.

This is what witnessing the world shows us. We do not procrastinate about applying an assigned polarity to an event. Witnessing does not care what one believes to be good or bad, black or white, positive or negative. These are the products of involvement and attachment to meaning. Into the world of witnessing, there is only the observation of Isness: Everything simply is and need not be anything else other than what is.

When you are in the alignment of witnessing, you could imagine yourself as being transparent to the world. By existing in a mind without attachment, you are impervious to the karmic cycles that exist within the Isness of the world. There is only tranquil appreciation in the happenings of what you observe through the mind of your subconscious.

The World and Your World

There is a fundamental difference between existing in THE world, and existing within YOUR world. As stated, the world is meant to act as a realm of observation. Why is the word "meant" implied here? It's because many attempt to involve themselves with attempting to impact the world when this is simply not possible.

When you decide to exercise your passion to impact the world, such a thing cannot be accomplished. The idea of one person attempting to impact the nature of the world itself is no different than an ant trying to push down a vast skyscraper. The reason this intention becomes forged in many people's minds is because they see themselves separate from the world. They look at the world through their own meaning and immediately draw conclusions through polarized concepts believing the world must assemble to their own desire and demand. This belief is so powerful that they may spend the entirety of their lifetime struggling to push the current of nature to their will. Such an attempt is futile as nature does not conform to a fractional component of its own structure. Such a mentality of thinking could be compared to a small gear within an infinite machine that attempts to rebel and become the very machine itself.

As a human being, we represent a component that is part of the whole. A component cannot hold the power to manipulate the current of the whole world so it can conform to your desire. Such an endeavor would violate the universal law of free will. As free will exists, every being is naturally orientated to freely express themselves as a component within the collective will of the universal body.

Mankind has adopted the habit of holding a need to change so much of nature to suit its own standards. Our ability to create becomes misguided as we believe everything around us must be manipulated to make sense of it. The ability to create is to work through what surrounds us so that the inner power to perceive and manifest encourages growth within our being, never from without it. An aligned, expansive creator works through the flow of nature to see the living art that exists inside. That art becomes inspiration and a compliment to the stream of nature's energy becomes the expression of that creator: To plant a tree, to draw in the dirt, to use the colors of nature to create beautiful artwork, dancing to the sound of birds, singing songs of love throughout the lands of the Earth, building a home out of the Earth for your family to live. These are all powerful compliments to the energies of nature. Nature itself is not being challenged, but complimented. It is not being opposed, but allied with.

Such inspirations that encourage creativity that compliment nature comes from the very fabric of witnessing the world. Letting yourself be still so that the world before you can enact its actions. As you observe, you obtain inspiration. With inspiration, you return to your world and begin the creation process.

The world of humanity, nature and the Earth is only meant to be witnessed as a reflection of your own subconscious inner clockwork. That world on a collective level cannot be altered by any means. Conserve your energies and let that realization be clear to you. Take what you can observe from the collective witnessing and let it inspire you to become a prime example of what you wish to create within your own world. This will lead us into the discussion of the next world that holds crucial life messages for us to consider: The Dream World.

In Review...

- The collective world is a looking glass and can only be observed, never altered by you.

- Focus on your world to see the greatest changes happen as this is the world that you will always interact with.

CHAPTER 12
THE DREAM WORLD

The two worlds we are most familiar with: the physical world and the dream world. One world includes boundaries that limits our abilities to express ourselves, restricts our capabilities as beings physically and mentally and isolates us upon laws governed through space, time and matter. The other world holds no limits to the first whatsoever. Anything goes for as deep and vast as our imaginations can allow. This is the dream world.

The world of dreams holds itself together as a grid of our own subconscious. Our perceptions within the awoken life slate its essence into existence. The definitions we assign through emotion within life will reflect on a much larger scale through the unlimited possibilities of the dream world.

Why Do We Dream?

The cause of dreams is quite simple to explain...

Karma creates dreams.

This is the only reason we dream. As discussed, karma represents the mediumship of memory and memory represents what we would understand as time. When one who commits their energies to working upon themselves from within transpires, they will find that they will require the experience of **karmic dreaming** less and less. This is replaced by the feeling of becoming fundamentally multidimensional and operating in many realities. You will exist in other realms simultaneously exploring the wonders of your reflections both when awake and asleep. It will no longer become a dream world, but a unified world where the dream is now your true reality.

The dreams we commonly experience are messages from our own spiritual selves. Our higher mind is attempting to convey messages to us as we assign definitions and meanings to the reflections we encounter within life. Dreams become surreal in their expression as they follow the law of free will. Answers are not given to one, but only symbolism, metaphors and imagery are the common language of the dream plane.

Such metaphorical imagery is needed because our own subconscious doesn't organize itself within the parable of space and time linearly. It is not the understanding of a single being who sits down with us and has a meaningful conversation about what we need to work on within ourselves. No, it's role, as stated before; is a grid. In other words: it is a hall of mirrors. It reflects our deepest emotional states without filters. It cares not for what we consider right or wrong. It only reveals truth about ourselves in the rawest ways possible unrestrained by sensitivity or forbearance.

Necessity of Dreams

Believe it or not, dreams are not produced via REM sleep. Dreams are a choice applied by each of us. They are a transmission source that interlocks with ourselves as we leave our bodies astrally each night. REM simply represents a state to where are receptively attuned to travel through the astral planes of existence. That explanation warrants the technicality to entering the dream plane, but that doesn't represent the necessity to dreaming whatsoever. Dreams are magnetically attracted to us as we are in receptive alignment via REM sleep. To enter dreams, our astral body fragments itself and splinters its array into hundreds, even thousands of projections. Think of it as a beam of light entering a multi-faceted crystal prism that divides and disperses many other beams of light to all corners of a room. This crystal prism is our own body.

When entering other dreams, there is no such thing as a beginning or end to the dream in question. You are contained within that reality to experience a crucial moment that holds importance to an emotional state reflecting to you.

Therefore, the necessity of dreams equates to the revisiting of the true self with the physical self. Nothing in all of creation is ever buried or removed. We take responsibility for every action, every expression and every experience in life and that impact is shown as result through ourselves within our dreams. Dreams are record keepers and emotional gauges. They keep score in a manner of speaking so that we realize the type of energies we attract and repel within reality. To put it simply, our dreams are necessary teachers for our own self/spiritual advancement. Without the structure of dreams to show us about ourselves and the emotions we portray, we cannot learn nor grow nor imagine. Only when self-realization, karmic alignment and personal surrender lead us into personal unification can the dream world merge with the physical world to become one.

Different Perspectives Within Dreams

Why is it that when we dream, we may appear as other people or other beings operating in another reality? Simply because the meaning of the emotional catalyst that attracts such a dream where you operate as another being best serves the message conveyed through that dream reality itself. Whether you are yourself, or within the body of a friend, a family member, an animal or just a floating observer of the dream, such a perspective holds merit to the vantage point in question.

Remember, dreams do not teach us through pep talks or lectures like what we may be accustomed to through a teacher or an authority in the physical world. They show us situations that give clear definitions of the types of feelings and emotions we claim due to the meanings we assign within our awoken reality.

For example, seeing yourself as an ant within a dream who suddenly gets squashed by an enormous boot could symbolize the imbalance of you seeing yourself as a great insignificance with little to no self-value whatsoever.

A second example could be seeing yourself as a magnificent bird beautiful in appearance whose wings have been clipped. You feel filled with sorrow as you fear you may never fly again. This symbolic imbalance shows that you have limitations imposed upon your freedom, and that you stay confined for the sake of others as your wings are clipped, not broken nor removed.

Dreams are telling us about ourselves through every type of perspective we can imagine. Unfortunately, many devalue dreams as being mere fantasy and do not take their messages to heart. As they remain oblivious to their dream messages, their lives continue to be saturated with conflict. Pain only continues through one's life and emotional whirlwinds intensify for if one continues to embrace the imbalanced meanings they imprint within life that they're dreams are revealing to them.

The Dream Samsāra: Resolving the Loops

Dreams take us into themes of our lives that are saturated with powerful emotions. As mentioned, dreams speak to us through these astral planes of reality showing us the deepest subconscious aspects of ourselves. These dreams can be both very inspiring and even quite frightening depending what we are holding onto emotionally.

One who is in a great deal of emotional pain will cycle through a Samsāra of dream themes that are speaking about what the dreamer is constantly holding onto. This loop will reproduce itself in different 'canvases' through our nightly dream state, but the messages will remain the same.

The action of breaking the loop and exploring different areas of your subconscious will come more often through awoken revelations. For example, one who may experience great fear running from an unknown beast deep in the heart of dark woods is experiencing a fear of their own self. There are elements of fear that relate to abandonment or rejection that fuel this unknown beast who can be heard roaring and tromping in the background of this dream. The sound starts to get closer, but the beast cannot be shown. It's within that moment where the roar becomes the loudest and the dreamer awakens that something triggers within their mind. Realization visits them and they suddenly recognize what that beast is: their lack of acceptance of their self. It is the emotional power of rejection, abandonment and judgment that they have placed on themselves. Once this realization is felt, the dream has done its job in showing the dreamer what they've been holding onto for a great deal of time. The dreamer now understands the language of the dream and begins to apply actions in accepting themselves. Their reality shifts as they apply complimentary time that soothes and rests the emotional imbalance. They've accepted the emotional pain, forgiven it and will now liberate from it as they empower themselves with the positive reinforced feeling of freedom, joy and love.

As the dreamer continues to work on themselves through realization, the Samsāra loop breaks and new explorations within the dreamer's dream landscape can be explored reflecting the mirrors of their personal salvation and liberating feelings.

Emotions are the Fuel of Dreams

What we do not learn from will continue to repeat through the Samsāra of our life. We will continue to wander through the intense voltages of our emotional conflict until we see the boundaries of limitations by empowering such imbalanced distortions. Emotions are the most powerful extension of energy that exists within us and their illusions of confinement is highly alluring. Emotions want to be fueled repeatedly as they are the addiction to the programs of identity we have placed upon ourselves. Dreams are by far the greatest tool we can have to dissecting the subconscious mind and observing the entanglements of life seeded within the garden bed of ourselves. Therefore, it is wise to recall as much as your dream state each night as much as possible. Create a dream journal and empower your memory through meditative practices.

One example of a dream recall meditation can be:

Enter a relaxing space where you will not be disturbed. Turn off any distracting elements in your environment and focus upon being empty. Take deep cleansing breaths breathing in through the nose and out through the mouth. With each breath, feel yourself becoming more and more relaxed.

Enter a void within the mind that holds nothing distracting. Let your attention be focused entirely upon the void. Stay in this state for several moments as the breath guides you in maintaining a focus on emptiness.

Within the void, call upon the energies of your memory. See it in any form that it wishes to present itself. Consider its chosen form and send high vibrations of love to its essence. Imagine this love as crystal snowflakes entering the essence of memory. See how memory responds as you send pure love to it. Share a loving intention to your memory:

"I send infinite love to the totality of my memory. May its light be bright, its love be pure and its connection to my conscious self-aligned. May memory serve me well within my dream state this night as my intention to speak to my subconscious is paramount through my intent. I bless my memory. I bless my being. All is one, one is all. And so it is."

Stay within this space if you wish to empower your memory with these pure snowflakes crystallized from your love. You will intuitively know when it will be time to return to physical reality. The most important intention to be achieved is the love bonding between your memory and yourself. As you do this, you may be pleasantly surprised of how well your memory has improved. Not only through dream state, but within awoken life as well.

As you perform meditation exercises such as this, commit yourself to recording what memory wishes to share with you each night as you go to sleep. When awakening to document your dreams, it's important that you keep your subtle energies intact by not moving around too much or performing anything strenuous or intense. Stay afloat in subtle energy as this is how the dream world communicates with you. Gently reach for your dream journal or diary and just let the subtlety of memory guide your writing hand with what you recall within dream-time. Be as descriptive as you can and let memory lead the way. As you perform the meditation example or other meditations like its context each night, you'll notice that memory will have more to tell you each time you dream.

Methods to Interpret Dream Symbolism

When working with dream symbolism, once you get a fundamental understanding of the dream symbolism, the key to interpretation is being able to see the symbols in sequence. This would be no more different than studying tarot or oracle cards. It's not about one generic, defining symbol, but seeing how these sequences interact with each other.

For example, experiencing a dream where you are flying untethered. From Sigmund Freud's perspective, this could be defined as "sexual release." However, the key is not the generic definition, but the sequence of what comes before and after relating to symbolism to understand the dream overall.

If we were to dive deeper into this example, the dream may also incorporate a female seeing herself wearing a white dress and sailing through the air without restriction. She may also recall smiling and laughing while she flew through the clouds. These are important symbols that would represent breaking past barriers of personal restriction. The symbolism of the white dress could also symbolize feeling lighter and not having to carry anything heavy or restrictive. The color white is often represented as a color of freedom and purity. The smile and laughter is the reflection of her liberation past a belief that was once confining. So this is showing that it's not about one simple symbol that tells the entirety of the dream, it's about the sequence that tells the dreamer more about herself and what she has experienced as a reflection within her own subconscious.

In looking at dream symbols, look for the simplest explanation to determine its common meaning. But most importantly, see how the puzzle pieces of symbols connect through the sequence to find out deeper understandings regarding yourself in dream-time. It is through this tactic that you will find depth and a greater revealing of what your emotions are attempting to tell you.

In Review...

- Karma creates dreams.

- Dreams are emotional attractions.

- Surrender to the wisdom of your emotions to break the loops of recurring themes within dreams.

- Work with your memory to increase dream recall.

- Create a dream journal/diary.

- Explore the sequence of dream symbols, and not the symbols themselves to understand the depth of your dream and how it is portraying itself to you.

CHAPTER 13
THE LIVING LIBRARY OF EARTH

In this author's previous book, Rainbow Wisdom, the living library was defined as the Akashic Records where all knowing within the universe was stored. In this chapter, we're going to be looking more into the heart of accessing the universal insight through the essence of the library itself: Mother nature.

Intelligence is found within every living thing that we can imagine. From a grain of sand, to a passing cloud, the sky, and the Earth herself. The very existence of a living library is to access knowledge stored within living vessels to understand the fundamentals of creation.

Earth is an ancient world that has within itself this very living library where we do not just access ethereal information through our consciousness, but through the canvases of life that speak to us in an infinite amount of ways. As we've learned throughout this book, it is not about vocal dialogue, but feeling that is the universal language through all life that exists. Everything that is alive can interface with you so that they can show you their worlds within the heart of your own.

From the grass beneath your feet, the wood upon your hardwood floors, the cotton within your clothing, the leaf of lettuce in your salad and the coffee in your cup. These examples are living beings that can tell you a great deal about the living library of Earth.

The Heart of Knowledge

Through the living library of Earth, what is it to experience knowledge from other forms of life? The knowledge we experience is perspective. For this is all that knowledge truly is. Endless facets of perspective from one and another sharing unique truth on what the universe means to them. To have knowledge is to have meaning through a vantage point. Therefore, it is the idea that one grain of sand is being educated through all sorts of grains of sand scattered throughout a desert. That one grain sand is just as valuable, unique and treasured as any other grain because it too holds knowledge. The same goes for you. As a human being, you are a knowledge center. You contribute to the whole as a facet of life that makes the universe the beauty that it is.

Interfacing with the Library

Wherever you may be now reading this book, find something around you that is alive: a food item, a leaf, a clump of soil, a pebble, etc. Let yourself become clear and empty. Relax yourself and surrender to the beauty of this eternal moment of now.

As you relax and still your mind, take that form of life that is with you and place your hand(s) upon it. Listen to it. Feel what it is to be that form of life. What is its perspective? What knowledge does it wish to bestow upon you? What is its universal vantage point? Take a few moments and explore this unique form of life as the living will always communicate openly with the living. Remember that the greatest translation of communication comes through feeling. Let your heart be opened, let the mind be silent and just listen as you hold that form of life in your hand(s).

Now... what do your feelings tell you about that form of life? What did your heart translate to you as you held the life into your hands? If you felt something, then you are learning to sense strongly with your heart. If sensing is still a challenge for you, then you will want to spend more time opening your heart more by bringing more attention to your feelings. Your alliance with your feelings will allow your heart to open wide and this will elevate your awareness to that of a living librarian.

The Living Librarian

What is a living librarian? It is one who can see a world deeper than what the physical senses can interpret. It is one who can listen to all forms of life and share in their stories on how life chooses to exist as facets of the universe. A living librarian is a reality whisperer who experiences themselves through all things and functions as an interpreter to all forms of life. But most importantly, a living librarian is a creator. Through their ability to feel the knowledge of life flowing through them, their ability to create becomes greatly enhanced with perspectives of creative expressions. Therefore, Earth as a living library holds the most exceptional gift of all: us. We are the creators of the living library and there are no other such beings in the entire universe like the human being who has become a reality whisperer... a living librarian... a creator being.

Earth as a Living Library Planet

Our world is a unique one to say the least. Since its ancient times, it has been occupied by ancient astronaut settlers that have emerged from different dimensional realities. Each of these settlers were volunteers of a great experiment in seeding life from the vast depths of civilization that go beyond our local galaxy. It is this very reason that a vast variety of life exists upon this world. All life on this planet did not just become locally propagated. All life needed to be brought here from many other different civilizations that were passionate in contributing to the Earth living library project. From the flora and fauna of the plant and vegetation density, to the variety of life forms from: insects, fish, avian, reptiles, amphibians, mammals and then eventually... us.

Humanity is the newest archetype of life form on the planet because we have been assigned a very important duty: we are to be stewards of the Earth. Just as a gardener would keep the integrity of a garden intact and thriving with producing abundant harvests, we too are these living librarians who are designed to listen to life on the planet, care for the life and create innovations that will compliment life and the Earth as one.

The key to opening our capabilities as living librarians stems from our heart source. When you learn to listen to life as you did in the above example, you will see the nature of reality unfold in a very spectacular way. The depth perception of life will become grand and everything that you thought represented a materialized Earth will dissolve away as the true essence of the living library planet will become fully revealed to you.

This is what it is to understand the nature of the unit. It is not about mastering your physical senses, obtaining intellectual aptitude and reading every science book you can get your hands on. No. It is about being able to listen to the inner connections that exist within you. It is about being open to perspectives through all forms of life that you encounter. It is about understanding possibilities within yourself you never thought you could access. It is about functioning as a creator to compliment the cycle of life so that more life through design can be welcomed within this plane of existence with unbridled love.

When we access the living library of Earth, this is what we will learn. The Akashic Records holds perspective within every imprint of life, and the life upon this world holds a unique imprint where you can receive this expanse of knowledge. Perspective will visit you representing every living form that is your planetary companion.

In Review...

- Knowledge is perspective.

- All life upon the Earth can be accessed through your own sensitivity to personal feeling. The heart is the gateway to life interfacing.

- A living librarian is a creator being and we have been given the gift to create and compliment life as stewards of the Earth.

CHAPTER 14
THE DEATH PROCESS

Even though the understanding of death can be quite tragic with in our lives, it is for each of us to understand but the death process is helping to complement life.

The death process and understanding our own mortality is the greatest benefit on how life can reproduce itself through everything it has learned in previous incarnations that represent each of us. Although we are very connected to loved ones that have passed back into spirit, their essence will forever be a part of ourselves.

Life Reborn

Every time a physical body retires back into Source consciousness, the universe itself is receiving instructions on everything that represents that entity's memories. These memories that return to the oversoul are a compliment to life itself as the rebirth of life can now take place through the learning that the memories have provided. It is helpful to see the death process as a learning experience. Such a learning experience allows the universal construct to become refined. All the memories that we hold through the experience of life is all in all the catalyst to bringing us closer to wholeness.

Understanding the Death Process

There has never been a time when a soul has ever expired out of existence. Death can be commonly seen as this understanding. However, the true idea of death does not reflect such a concept in the least. There has never been any form of proof to confirm that death represents the end to one's awareness of existence. The soul is an infinite continuum of expression and can never cease to exist.

It is important to understand that death simply represents a boundary. When we are looking up the understanding of a boundary, it tells us of moving into a new form of transition. In other words, the death process is that of transformation and nothing more. Even though the bodies of Flesh may eventually expire, it has no form of detrimental consequence as it relates to your infinite existence. As we have explored in earlier chapters, the soul houses itself into a body to experience itself as an interface to engage in experiences that propagate memory. One may say that the aspects of memory created by experience is the true currency of the universe. Therefore, it is understandable to look at the universe as a vast database of knowledge content funneled through the perspectives of ourselves.

When we pass away, all this experience that we have culminated provides us with the opportunity to renew ourselves as a new form of life. This new form of life will once again be a part of the living matrix as we once again play the game of incarnation.

What Happens Through the Death Process?

When one passes away from the physical body, they return into the astral plane of existence. When existing in this realm, it is no more different then if you were to exist in the dream plane. It all depends on the soul that has discarnated from the body. If an entity holds a great deal of emotional pain within themselves, the experience inside this astral plane will allow such emotions to come to life more vividly than the physical plane. As we have discovered in previous chapters, emotion is a very powerful energetic. It is emotion itself that confine us within a reality based upon its meanings. Through this example, this is what can cause certain entities to experience a reality that could reflect a domain of hell. When one is at the mercy of their own emotions within this astral plane, they will continue to experience these emotions until they have been re-balanced. Fortunately, there are a variety of different spiritual helpers that exist within every plane of existence. These helpers are entities that work with other souls trapped in their own nightmares of emotions to bring them back into the light. This brings comfort as no matter how deep into darkness you may go through the onslaught of emotions, the light is always available to you so that you may return into your authentic self.

The Tunnel to the Oversoul

Very commonly, those who have had an out-of-body experience often witness what could be referred to as a tunnel of light. The purpose of this tunnel of light is very like what we could refer to as a soul memory vacuum. The soul moves up this tunnel and returns into the parent soul so that the memories may become one with that very parent soul. Such a soul is referred to as the oversoul. The responsibility of the oversoul is to harvest memory from its children souls and share these memories with the universal matrix. In other words, the oversoul could represent a type of buffer that feeds the information from souls Into the heart of the universe itself so that the universe can reflect on these memories as a way to improve itself infinitely.

Life Review

After moving up this tunnel of light, many experience the opportunity to review the highlights of their own life. These life highlights are snippets of our own lifetime that help us to understand that challenges and revelations that have been associative with strong emotion so that we can reflect on what has truly impacted us through this lifetime. Did we help enough people? Did we work to help ourselves? Did we contribute love to others? Did we withhold love from ourselves? Where there is imbalance emotionally, we will feel this imbalance as it affects everybody that we have met that also shares in the effect of this emotional outcome.

In other words, you may feel the pain of others that have received the ripple effect of this powerful emotional instability and you will see how it affected them personally. However, it is important to understand that all the healing that we do here in this lifetime can be resolved without having to feel it in an exceptionally powerful way through the life review. The purpose of the life review is not to torture you, but only to show you what has been withheld through your neglect to bring self-reflection and healing to yourself. This is another reminder on how important this moment in your life is. In this very moment now, you can cleanse yourself of all emotional imbalances so that's your life review can reflect your triumph and elevations to higher planes of existence that reflect the love within you.

Other Versions of Death

You understand now that the death process is a boundary for transformation. In seeing it in this form, this is showing you that you've died quite often. When an old Paradigm belief system has been rendered invalid, everything that represented that old paradigm is a death process birthing a brand-new version of you. Many of the ancient teachers encourages to go into these frequent aspects of death so that we can peel away the layers that no longer serve us upon our path to True authenticity.

For example, if you have felt like you have withheld love because you have not felt loved yourself, realization visits you through the emotions that you have withheld and the emotions no help to show you what has been buried with him. Having this realization, you understand that love is valid in your life. This new understanding has allowed the old emotional imbalance of withholding love to die. It has done so because it is no longer a theme that represents yourself. Every time you heal emotional imbalance that you find within yourself personally, you have experienced the death process and have become something more to the essence of true authenticity.

Like everything that we have learned in this book, see the death process as your greatest ally. Just because one retires from the physical body that can no longer function, that will never mean that it is the end of you or someone you love. As the death process has reveal to you, life only transforms. It can never cease to exist as it is infinite as existence itself.

Celebrating Life

It is very common for us to mourn a loved one who has passed away. Many of us may feel empty and disconnected without their physical presence. The passing of their physical body makes us feel that we are being left behind and abandoned. When we grieve for loved ones who have passed, we are causing them a great deal of pain because they feel guilty in returning to the light. It is understandable when someone who we care about greatly is no longer present with us. But as we have observed through this book, nothing never ceases to exist. The greatest compliment you can give to a loved one who has passed away is celebrating the memories that they have shared with you in a lifetime that reflects profound love. Let the tears that you feel be the tears of joy in appreciation for a soul that has never turned back into their infinite construct. When you send a great deal of love to that entity, they will no longer feel tethered by the emotions of others and feel guilty in returning to the light. When we celebrate one's life we feel the joy that is contained within ourselves because we attracted such a person into our lives that has shown the beauty that we are. The path of celebration is what blooms greater opportunities of existence that show us a broader perspective through the continuum of life itself.

In Review...

- Death has nothing to do with a ceasing of existence.

- Death is a boundary leading to transformation.

- Be aware of your emotions as they will become a vivid part of your reality when you pass from the physical body.

- When you heal old paradigms, you will become renewed and have experienced a death process.

- Celebrate the life of another who has returned to the realm of spirit. Your love encourages them to return to their infinite construct.

CHAPTER 15
THE HUMAN WILL

One of the greatest components we have as human beings is the ability of possessing will. In ancient times, there were stories of many different mystical beings that were born of fire or acted as forces of nature. We can refer to such beings as Djinn, Elementals or the Fae. But through these different beings, none of them are capable of holding will. Will is an ability reserved only for a creator being. Yes... a living librarian.

With many ancient astronauts that have visited our world throughout many millennia who were talked about in ancient writings and drawings, even they could not equal the power of will that the human being holds. They were knowledgeable, intellectual and possessed incredible technology. Many of these ancient astronauts taught us how to write, explore mathematics, grow food and function as a growing civilization. But as they saw the power that the human will had, they were amazed as they knew that even their civilizations could not even come close to the potential creative power of humanity. For it was us that were the avatars. We were the deities wearing human garments that could project the potentials we had through the innovations and inceptions that came to us. The human being is the most advanced biological vessel ever created. We can shift through the entire contrast of the spectrum of expression with ease. Our hunger to learn and improve ourselves is second to none. To pull ideas out of thin air and hold the will to bring it into being shows our promise of being these prolific creator beings. We are the most willful beings in all the universe.

The Power of Will

Will itself truly has no direct definition. One can only approximate a translation for something that is completely intangible. It is our drive to succeed, our passion to create, our spirit shining when inspired. It is a creational ray that projects itself when we become committed to an inception. It is the power of the universe itself funneled through the vessel of a creator being propagating manifestation facilitated through the intention of love. To define will is something best described by poets and philosophers because logic itself is not involved in harnessing the potential of our will. It is empowered through feelings of passion and dedication. To express will is no different than an artist picking up a brush, choosing their colors of paint and creating a masterpiece upon a canvas that becomes their reality.

Will and Equivalent Exchange

Such beings like the Djinn, the Elementals and the Fae could be defined as immortal beings. Why is this? It's because these beings have no influence over the essence of creation. Their presence is as a force of nature and they are only capable of manipulating what has already been created. It is impossible for such beings to create something new or invent something completely original. No. These beings can only rearrange and act as such forces that can steer or redirect the energies of nature. The cost for obtaining immortality is observation from creation. To create in our plane of existence, mortality is the cost so that creativity can grow, evolve and change. This is the price that is granted through one of the universal laws: Equivalent exchange. As we are governed to work within this law, this is what nature lives by.

A human can never be immortal. There will come a time where life can be prolonged and we have more time to express ourselves on deeper levels as we develop a certain level of physical, mental and emotional maturity. Nonetheless, the body will eventually expire and our opportunities to create within this plane will extinguish like the passing of a season.

Reaching Willful Maturity

The ability to create is the most powerful ability there is to have. It is important that the act of creating is used responsibly. Where one or many may abuse creation to create immaturely where manifestations are forged to harm or mislead others, this leads to a shortening of life as the concept of creativity becomes more materially felt than spiritually felt. It is this very reason why human beings may only live an average of 70=80 years; whereas in the bible, human beings lived well over 600 years.

Materialized creation shortens the lifespan because of the allure of dependability upon the physical life. There is less care and appreciation to the natural energies that exist within the body and in nature. Where that is being neglected in creativity, such negligence leads to a resulted effect to the reducing of lifespan. Where this is being collectively felt, most the population will attract situations in their lives where environmental contamination and abuse towards the self becomes manifest. This is the reason why our planet has been polluted, our food is being poisoned, our air and water is becoming contaminated. We have functioned for too long upon the reliability of creating technology over creating will to expand and empower our natural consciousness capabilities.

When a society decides to cast off the dependability of material technology and return to the roots of co-existing with nature, our natural health physically, mentally and emotionally dramatically changes. The populace now works in harmony with their natural surrounding environment. Many now start to deeply appreciate their bodies, their minds and their hearts. Harmony is established in working alongside the Earth and will is now put in its authentic place: creating contributions to aid, complement and expand living potential through the vast capabilities discovered within nature.

When we move into this perception, the human life expectancy will radically improve through each generation. Even though we still exist in mortal form, the longevity to create in such a form will be far more grand and expansive as we see worlds unfolding that will take our civilization ahead to the point of god-like potential. That's how powerful humanity is. We are literally gods in training due to the creative capability of contrast we naturally possess. All it takes to harness it is our ability to go within, surrender ourselves and let the will within us shine. As we shine, we become further interconnected with our world around us.

Aligning to Your Will

To work with your will is to take your empowerment and make it your greatest ally. Your will is the pinnacle essence of your intention. The will to act, the will to create, the will to manifest and the will to receive. Will allows your greatest passions to come to life. To understand is to acknowledge what means the most to you through the path of least resistance. What is something that excites that you know you have the will to act on? Start with that intention and let will guide you as you immerse within that intention and make it your world.

As you work through the path of personal will, you will see how simple it will become. Let the actions of will become branded with possibility in your mind and follow through with it. All possibilities exist through you if you hold willful value through all that you choose to experience. Where there in invalidation, there is magnetic repulsion as you have not given yourself permission to pursue such a world that the invalidation represents. In time, that can be adjusted; but focus on what serves you here and now and stretch out with your will magnetizing the intentions you hold capability with here and now.

Understanding the Impossible

The impossible is and always shall be a label of what can't currently be perceived due to invalidation. Nothing within all of creation is impossible. When one's will is prominent enough, the acting of will shall break past all boundaries to make that aspect of conception real in some form within your world of experience.

When we truncate our capabilities by drowning them in an ocean of belief, we live in the world of the impossible. Your belief system barriers are impenetrable for as long as you value them. No one can shape, alter or break you from these barriers. You are the creator of your own universe, and in being so, all boundaries you erect will become permanent until you decide otherwise. This is what grants the impossible into being: belief.

When one is empty and neutral to all beliefs and concepts, the impossible can no longer exist. You have dissolved all the walls, barriers and barricades preventing you from fully expressing yourself. Therefore, the impossible no longer holds substance. As you exercise your will, be empty of barriers and fluidic in adaptability. As you do, the universe will speak to you with possibilities your imagination could never conceive. That is the power of will within you.

In Review...

- The human being is the most powerful creator in the universe.

- Will holds all capabilities and it is up to you to decide where you wish to direct it through your own validation.

- Human are mortal beings with the ability to infinitely create. This is the result of equivalent exchange.

- Those that choose immortality cannot create in this realm, they can only manipulate.

CHAPTER 16
THE LIGHT BODY

The light body would be defined as the closest understanding to our natural selves. Our matrix as a being is comprised of a spirit, mind and body. The aspect of the light body shows our true form with the physical layers removed. It is the luminous body that occupies the astral plane and more of it becomes known in higher planes of existence. Is such planes, we are no longer the accumulation of a body, but the totality of light and consciousness itself.

Working with the light body, we can develop a symbiosis with this form that can grant us interdimensional travel to other worlds beyond our own.

Firstly, to understand the light body, we will look deeper into the chakra seals contained within our physical body.

The Chakra Seals

The chakra seals aren't placed within the physical body, but they share the same space as it were. There won't be a deep focus on the basic discourse as chakras are quite commonly well known.

To summarize, chakras reflect the rainbow spectrum bands and station themselves within the base of the spine, navel, solar plexus, heart, throat, brow and the crown of the head.

The chakras operate as seals that allow the soul to incarnate into the body through different layers of the reality spectrum operating in full capacity with the physical realm. Each chakra seal has its own specific nature and orientation as it reflects the seven astral layers of the body.

Root chakra represents stability and structure.

Sacral chakra represents sexuality and relationships.

Solar plexus chakra represents self and wellbeing.

Heart chakra represents connection and feeling.

Throat chakra represents truth and expression.

Third eye chakra represents the inner self and insight.

Crown chakra represents spiritual connection and natural order.

The chakras are essential for one to fully incarnate through ensoulment into the body. Those who possess strong clairvoyance can often see the chakra seals diminish when one has passed from the body and back into spirit.

In conclusion, the chakras are spiritual seals that contain us within a physical form and operate within a spectrum of reality. They are also receivers and are translating the experiences of ourselves back into the heart of our oversoul parent.

Working with the Light Body

We have reviewed the functioning of the chakra centers because this a process that will be duplicated when you learn how to construct your own replicant light body. This exercise will be available in the next chapter.

Like our own physical body that contains spirit seals within itself, we have the capability of duplicating this process as we create a body that exists within the astral realm that our consciousness can occupy.

The light body has no real form: It is luminous, timeless, and spaceless. It can anywhere, anything and anyone. As our consciousness is as infinite as creation itself, we can anchor a fraction of our conscious self into such a body and explore any aspect of the universe we desire.

The exercise in the next chapter will teach you how to create a light body form that will appear as physical as yourself. It will also teach you about chakra seal placement and using an altar. The altar will serve as an anchorage point where you can consciously astral project your consciousness into the Earth's physical plane.

Exploration with the Light Body

Once you learn how to construct your own light body, you will need to become more accustomed in developing your inner senses so that you can experience it vividly. It is not about having only clairvoyance, but being able to replicate your physical senses with your astral senses: sight, hearing, smelling, touch, tasting. This is a technique that requires continual practice, so don't feel discouraged if you're not able to experience it fully right away.

Generating a light body consciousness gives us an extension of exploration both within our own physical world and worlds beyond. Imagine walking upon the surface of another planet and observing ancient ruins left behind by extraterrestrial races. Or visiting other star systems where you can fly by planets and feel the collective energy of other populaces that exist there. Or moving into deeper dimensional realms where you can experience structures comprised entirely out of light where luminous spiritual beings greet you.

The Altar

The altar functions like a beacon when you begin to construct your light body. The altar is only necessary if you wish to anchor your body into your physical concurrent reality. If you wish to perform extradimensional exploration, one will not be needed.

Using a conjured or intuitively-received symbol will be the anchor point for your altar. This will lead to the symbol being aligned and bonded to the energies of a pentagram representing connection to the five elements within nature.

Afterwards, a circle is created either physical or within the mind that represents the radius in which the light body can exist within. This is a common practice that exists through many wiccan and pagan rituals as it relates to an altar.

Once you have configured your altar appropriately, you may begin the exercise in generating your light body. Remember that a light body can be of any appearance you wish. The most important thing is learning to function within your light body. One may wish to simply replicate their own form of self-identity within a light body and become used to basic functioning as it pertains to motor functions. But feel free to use your imagination and explore many facets of yourself.

To conjure different appearances of yourself, you must be aware of how those forms behave. Like in elemental magick, one must be immersed within the feeling of the elements to grasp their function and purpose. The same would apply to any creature or form you wish to appear as. Imagine what it is to be a butterfly or a small lizard. Study their functions and behavior and replicate it for yourself. This helps you to understand different facets of expression as an infinite being of creation.

The Oversoul of Your Light Body

Constructing your light body also gives you a strong understanding of how the oversoul functions. For example, if you have already constructed your light body and can materialize yourself vividly upon another plane of existence, you will instantly obtain all the memories of that experience until you dematerialize the body. This is identical to what the oversoul experiences. When a body passes, your projection of consciousness moves up a white tunnel and all memories of that life follow you leading into your life review as described in the death process chapter. Only In this instance, a life review is not necessary as you represent the oversoul of this projection. You serve as a witnessing observer experiencing your light body projection's interactions. This can teach you a great deal of the perspectives between involvement and observation.

In Review...

- The chakra seals are what contain us into our physical bodies so that we can interact in a physical spectrum of reality.

- The light body exists beyond the dimensions of space, time and matter.

- Your light body can be of any construct you wish if you become familiar with the form.

- An altar is used only for allowing your light body to function in your concurrent physical reality.

- You can function as the oversoul for your light body projection and obtain its memories in other realms of existence.

CHAPTER 17
SELF-EXPLORATION EXERCISES

This chapter will focus on several exercises that reflect on many concepts discussed within this book. Please ensure that you fully read the exercise before commencing it.

The Preparation Exercise

Please repeat this exercise before commencing any other in this chapter.

Find a space where you will not be disturbed. Ensure that you're comfortable and you may either sit or lay down for each exercise.

Lower the light level in your room if possible to encourage relaxation. Close your eyes and being to take deep cleansing breaths. Breathing in through the nose, and breathing out through the mouth. Repeat this rhythm of breathing a total of five times.

After your cleansing breaths, sit quietly as you center yourself through your natural breathing for approximately two minutes before commencing your intended exercise.

#1 - The Inner Child Exercise

Go into void. In this state, think back to yourself as a young child. Observe your innocence. Do not concern yourself with any memories that do not serve innocence in this state. Simply observe your youth and free-spirited nature. Become the younger version of you as you observe your inner child.

What does it feel like to be your younger self again? How free do you feel? How strong has your imagination become? Remember not to dwell on anything past or future that may cause disturbance. You are your inner child, and in being so, you are very present as well as playful.

Unleash the child's imagination. See beautiful worlds that come alive before your eyes. Focus on play and excitement. Be the essence of a child and let yourself become completely free. Let your world speak to you and feel that splendor of youthfulness once again. You have become wiser throughout your adult years. Focus on more fun and make this moment your second childhood. Reflect on this way of behaving today and unleash your inner child as you dedicate this day to play, excitement and presence.

#2 – Intuitive Strengthening Exercise

In this exercise, include a photo or written name of a friend, acquaintance or coworker. Find someone who is associated with you but whom you may not know too well.

Our intention in this exercise is only to observe the surface feelings of the individual. We are not probing deeply into their heart as such an action would require permission.

Simply sit with this photo or written name that conjures an image of the individual in your mind. Place all of your focus within your heart and simply observe the photo, or the image within your mind.

How are they feeling right now in this moment?

What do their surface thoughts tell you about them?

What do you feel you can do to help them feel loved and appreciated?

Meditation on these questions for a time. Do not feel that you need to answer them immediately. The intention of this exercise is to further open your feeling centers. More specifically: your heart space.

Attempt this exercise with others in your life repeating the same questions to yourself. Let your heart open wide as you sense their surface feelings and thoughts as well as how you would like to assist them.

Finally, focus on yourself. Be mindful of what your surface feelings and thoughts are telling you. How would you like to help yourself today? What do you feel you would like to do for yourself to feel personally loved and appreciated? Be honest with yourself and make yourself available for you here and now.

#3 – Intuitive Receiving Exercise

Enter void. Imagine that a beam of white light is entering your crown chakra. See your crown chakra opening wide like a thousand-petal lotus flower. Let this sensation stay with you for a few moments.

Through the connection of the white light, state your intention that you would like to intuitively receive (a symbol to enhance your mind/body abilities, connecting to a spirit guide, healing on a mental/emotional/physical level, etc.). Once you have shared your intention, see your body now being covered with a soft, white ethereal egg.

As this egg covers you, imagine your astral eyes are opening. Let the soft color of white function as a viewing screen for you. Here, you will receive images, symbols, words, feelings and/or sensations.

For example, if you set the intention to receive a symbol for healing, see it coming to you. If you have difficulty seeing it, feel it come to you. Know that you have received this symbol. After your exercise is complete draw out that symbol and meditate upon it in silence as this has been intuitively received by you. Follow your intuitive instincts and you will know what to do with what you receive intuitively.

#4 – Constructing the Light Body Exercise

Please ensure that you have an altar available for this exercise. Ensure that it is decorated using the four elements and contains a pentagram or pentacle in the center of it. Explore more on setting up altars in common wiccan practices as this will be acceptable for this exercise.

Repeat the intuitive receiving exercise as you use the beam of white light to receive a symbol that will allow your light body to co-exist within your physical plane. Once you have received your symbol, draw it out and place it in the center of the altar above the pentagram/pentacle.

Begin by creating a magick circle around the altar or create an ethereal magick circle within your mind. Let the circle surround your local environment (apartment, house, street, etc.)

In your mind, draw the five-pointed star pentagram within this circle. Bless the pentagram and the circle with the love of the five elements. This will fuse your magick circle into your reality plane and ensure that it holds a loving vibration of energy. Take a few moments to also bless your physical surroundings with your love.

Be in void. Bring your seven chakras into awareness through your body. As you see all seven chakras, imagine that you are dividing your luminous body from your physical body. See your luminous body directly in front of you with the seven chakra seals contained within it.

Give the intention to create a form through your luminous body. Remember that you should be familiar with the form you create prior to creating it through the light body. After you have given your body a form, invoke the magick circle in the void through intention and see/feel it upon the ground within your mind.

As you have materialized the magick circle within your space, see a beam of white light that is entering your crown and the crown of the light body. Give the intention to connect your consciousness with the vessel of your light body. As this is transpiring, begin to feel yourself within the light body looking back at your physical body in front of you. Take this time to acquaint yourself with calibrating the motor functions of the light body. Move your arms and fingers around. Wiggle your toes and try standing up and sitting back down. The most important part is that you are vividly seeing and/or feeling these actions.

After you have calibrated your light body, see a large ethereal egg of soft white light that is surrounding you and your physical body. See this ethereal egg transform into a domed soft wall of light surrounding you.

As this dome appears, imagine that your physical body is fading out from the realm. It is still there but it is now concealed so you can experience your light body.

The next step will depend if you wish to enter your concurrent physical reality, or if you wish to explore extra-dimensional realms. If you wish to enter concurrent physical reality, follow the next step. For extra-dimensional travel, skip the next step and proceed onto the next after.

Concurrent Reality Procedure

See the symbol that you created for the altar directly in front of you. See your light body extend a tether from your naval (like an ambilocal cord) to the center of the symbol. Take a few moments and feel the physical space where the symbol and the alter is located. As you feel this, give the intention to enter inside the magick circle you created.

Vividly witness the space you occupy and explore the space further.

Note: The more deeply relaxed you are, the more vivid this experience will feel to you. Do not attempt to think what you may see or feel, but allow the senses to be intuitively stimulated as you walk around with your light body. Again, this may take some practice before you're able to feel full vivid effects.

Within this environment, you can only experience what you have sealed within the magick circle. Proceed to the Conclusion procedure step.

Extra-Dimensional Travel Procedure

Through the beam of white light penetrating your crown, give an intention on where you would like to explore. You will not require the construction of a magick circle in extra-dimensional travel as that would require familiarity of a location. In this state, you can will any location as you experience it as an observer. See the beam of white light as an intelligent guide. It is singularity guiding you through the universe and can take you on a grand tour leading to open exploration. Remember that nothing can harm you within this state as you have blessed your space with loving intent.

Conclusion Procedure

Once you have finished exploring through your light body, say within your mind: "Return." You will now return into the void space. Send your loving intentions to all the energies you have worked with this day and see the beam of white light retracting itself back into the infinite. See your physical body return directly in front of you. Give the intention to return to your physical body.

As you re-enter your physical body, take a few moments to take deep breaths in and out and ground the memories you have received from exploration. See the light body phase out of being as you return yourself back into physical reality.

The more you continue to practice this technique, the stronger the vividness will become each time.

CONCLUSION

Your journey in discovering yourself as a steward of the Earth, a living librarian and a reality whisperer will continue past these finite pages. The essence of what can make you a refined human being is your ability to be in alliance with yourself. We all experience challenges within ourselves and with the external world, but if we possess the ability to befriend those challenges, learn from them, love them and release them; we will become these very stewards, librarians and reality whisperers.

Your body is the totality of reality itself. You are far more than what they physical body grants you as you may already be aware by reading this book. The strength comes from making our inner senses as strong as outer ones and learning to experience reality in a whole new way... the true way: from within.

What makes the journey easier is our adoption of self-appreciation and self-honoring. Respect, love and appreciate yourself each day. Open your heart up and value the feelings you experience regarding every situation you attract.

Emotions are the gauge that are offering the opportunity for correction and re-alignment. Respect those emotions. Do not attempt to change them, bury them or run from them. Let them speak to you and express them as they need to be expressed. Release them in peace and in love and may they leave you in harmony. Only then, can you attract what you now know you're worthy of. This is the prime result in helping you become this very steward of the Earth.

Continue to read this book over again. Like the previous book, Rainbow Wisdom; the words are intuitively guided to awaken realization within you.

Where you see challenge, welcome it. Where you see confusion, offer it kindness. Where others suffer, bring love into their world. Remember that struggle is just an adjustment of clarity waiting to happen. It invites you to look inside yourself and see the walls that you've erected. By embracing your shadows of emotion, this is what we'll welcome the greatest rays of light.

Your course to becoming a reality whisperer is already set. But it's not about the title; it's about the feeling. Liberation is the greatest gift you can give yourself. When you are free of emotional confinements, the world you thought you knew will never be a part of your reality again. More will be revealed to you and you will be in the alignment of a creator being. This is the path that each of us has set out to explore. There is no need for fear when you exist to see the many facets of yourself. You will always be the journeyer. We exist to connect, commune, integrate and expand ourselves. To have such intentions is to be a being created from love.

Thank you for being a part of this journey and exploring the infinite vastness of you. In time, you will see potentials within yourself guiding you into a new experience where you give reinvention to the real.

May it be well with you in all ways, dear reader.

Brad Johnson.

Visit our website:

www.RealityWhisperer.com

Made in the USA
San Bernardino, CA
07 January 2017